WORTH

A Story of Favor and Forgiveness

D1225508

WORTH

A Story of Favor and Forgiveness

ANN CHAMPION SHAW

gatekeeper press
Columbus, Ohio™

WORTH: A Story of Favor and Forgiveness

Published by Gatekeeper Press
2167 Stringtown Rd, Suite 109
Columbus, OH 43123-2989
www.GatekeeperPress.com

Library of Congress Control Number: 2021942037

ISBN (paperback): 9781662916663
eISBN: 9781662916670

"Surely Goodness and Mercy shall follow me all the days of my life."

—Psalm 23:6f

To

My mother who thought her
pictures were worth saving

And

My father who thought his words
were worth giving

TABLE OF CONTENTS

———————

FOREWORD

WORTH: A Story of Favor and Forgiveness is a rare treat for the person who has no predisposed attitude about finding, knowing and living your worth. Usually, books about self-journeying can feel sappy, arrogant or boring. We have read so many that we think we know the script. It usually contains a problematic childhood, abuse or abandonment, a period when the person experiences being lost, and then some crystallization event, salvation, forgiveness, or reconciliation to the people who wounded you, to yourself and to God.

WORTH includes some of these events, but the journey is not presumptive. It is a story that allows us to laugh, sing, cry and celebrate the life of a sister whose transparency and honesty is refreshing without being sappy.

I have known Rev. Ann Champion Shaw for years and have great respect for the excellence of her leadership, deep spirituality, and witness. She is an amazing woman who does amazing things. Her life mirrors that of so many people, including mine, which made reading WORTH so remarkable.

WORTH is not one of those tell-all books, written to grip your heart or make you wonder if the person has actually experienced healing. It is reflective, and inspiring as each chapter is named after an African American television show, which makes you start humming the theme song while you enjoy the read.

Included in WORTH are the principles of turning forward, looking back, celebrating life and family, finding yourself in the pain, and the victory in the journey. You are reminded you have worth in God from the beginning of your formation in God's thought.

WORTH is more than reading about Rev Ann's journey, it is reaffirming that your own worth is not defined by someone else, life circumstances, or your own mishaps. Worth is always defined by you and God. WORTH is a must read for this truth.

Anne Henning Byfield,

Bishop, African Methodist Episcopal Church

PICTURE THAT PREFACE

F red R. Barnard once said, "a picture is worth a thousand words," but one can argue that its value is much more as it speaks to life that is captured in its purest essence at a given moment. This is especially true when it comes to pictures of birthdays, graduations, vacations, weddings, and anniversaries that hold some of our most precious memories. Frozen in time, its image preserves the current space of its location, setting, culture, fashion, and attitude, showing "who we were" and "where we were" but not "who we will become." Besides, at the time any picture is taken, it shares no details about the future and speaks only to the present, leaving its participants in mystery that is privy only to the mind of the Divine. The connection and collision with self, family, and the world from that moment on is undetermined and waits invisibly in the background. It is only in the continuum of everyday life events, situations, and circumstances that goes beyond the print where the photographed will find the courage to face their future while enduring the hardest of times and rejoicing in the better ones. This is the case for the outside cover picture that portrays me and my siblings in December of 1979. My story, my truth, will begin with events from this day.

The GOOD TIMES

In 1979, Jimmy Carter was the president of the United States, Sister Sledge's "We Are Family" was at the top of the music charts along with James Cleveland's Gospel classic "God Is". *Star Trek: The Motion Picture* premiered on the big screen, and one of the most famous faces on television, acclaimed actress Esther Rolle, arrived at St. Mark in Orlando, Florida.

It was a beautiful Sunday morning in December where her regal presence made for an early Christmas present. As a child who usually sat closely by my mother and First Lady of St. Mark, Annie C. White Champion, I remember watching Rolle walk casually down the aisle wearing a hunter green dress, gold necklace, and donning her signature low 'fro. She wasn't surrounded by security nor an entourage of family and friends. Rolle was "Queen Esther" as she moved alone with grace, class, and style. It was her iconic role as the mother on *Good Times*, which spoke to the plight of an African American family residing in a Chicago Housing Project, that won her popularity and fans from all over the world.

Ms. Rolle, a native of Pompano Beach, FL, was a Golden Globe Award nominee for Best Actress and a Primetime Emmy Award winner. Her legendary role on *Good Times*, which just completed its final season, made her presence quite a stir, even in church. St. Mark tried to keep calm and not appear star struck, but one could easily see whispers in the choir, pulpit, as well as the congregation in efforts to verify her identity.

All the while, Rolle remained a QUEEN—poised and graceful with a sweet smile as she sat towards the front on the end seat, closest to the middle aisle. Peeking across Mother's shoulder to get a glimpse, I waved. She gave eye contact, smiled, and nodded her head. Then, I searched for my siblings, who sat towards the back of the church, catching eye contact with my big brother, George, as we both shared the look of amazement. Turning back around to face the pulpit, I was grinning from ear to ear when my father, Rev. George L. Champion Sr., the senior pastor, made the BIG announcement.

"Yes, we have a celebrity among us. Ms. Esther Rolle is here and she will come and offer a few words to us this morning."

The congregation roared in praise as she made her way to the podium to give remarks.

She was charming and brief as she spoke of how blessed she felt to be in Worship with us.

Afterwards, she returned to her seat while Father made a point to say, "Don't crowd her now, or stare too hard. Give her space. Besides, we're still in church."

St. Mark continued on in its normal, charismatic style of worship. With a packed church, great sounds from the choir, and powerful preaching, Rolle knew she was in the right place and would show evidence of it by nodding her head to the music and the Word.

"Is she going to eat with us today, Mama?" I asked.

"We'll see… I'll ask her after church," Mother replied.

After extending the invitation, Ms. Rolle said, "I don't want you all to have to go through any trouble just for me."

Mother replied, "Oh, no trouble at all! We would love for you to come over and dine with us. Everything is ready." Mother was right. With her and Father, everything was always READY.

At this point, Mother and Father had built one of the largest black churches in the State of Florida by erecting a new sanctuary, fellowship hall and a thriving Day Care and Head Start Program. Mother would often say, "It took prayers, blood, sweat, and tears to build St. Mark!" This phrase was likened to Moses in the Bible. Before entering the promised land, Moses faced many challenges in convincing the Israelites to trust God in the wilderness.

St. Mark was their promised land as young progressive blacks moved to Orlando for Disney World and the booming job market. In seeking a spiritual refuge, they would join St. Mark. Many would come being drawn to the soulful, gospel sounds of the choir, warm spirit of the people, and the charismatic preaching of Father. When the Holy Spirit would move upon persons' hearts, some would come down the long red-carpet aisle crying, others would come shouting, and even a few would come dancing.

In the end, they would shake Father's hand, while he offered his signature line, "JUST KNOW IN YOUR LIFE, THE BEST IS YET TO COME!" The best was happening in the life of St. Mark and the queenly presence of Esther Rolle was evidence of it.

* * *

Our home was known as "The Big House" because it was the largest and most distinctive in the Richmond Heights neighborhood, with its red brick exterior and two-car garage. When Ms. Rolle entered our "castle" with navy blue vinyl flooring, she was greeted by the pleasant aroma coming from the kitchen. She then stepped down into the sink-in dining room, which served as a hosting area for family and guests. Associate ministers and other invited guests came through to greet her in the lovely home that Mother designed alongside the architects.

Rolle's disposition remained the same—sweet, calm, and classy. We swarmed around her like bees as she spoke with my siblings and myself. She was especially drawn to my older sister Tymy's vibrancy, like most were, as Tymy (pronounced *Tie me*) boldly engaged Rolle with conversation. Tymy's beautiful mind closely examined any and all details of her environment which caused her to "pour the questions" on Ms. Rolle, who gladly responded.

We were all in awe of Rolle's presence and larger-than-life personality. Up to this point, I had only seen her as an image on our television set. Now, she was live and in-person, casually walking through our home. As other guests were engaging her in conversation, our family continued to pour on the hospitality just like we did with other guests who had come to our home before.

Church leaders, dignitaries, political heads, neighbors, and friends would come to the parsonage. Usually, the dining situation would be arranged with the adults eating at the big table in the dining room while the children would eat at the small table in the living room. We would often hear hot topics coming from the big table, which included church politics, world politics, social commentary, etc. The conversation would echo throughout the house and my father's loud volume would be in the center of it all. There were also the jokes, sometimes racy, which he told with an infectious laugh that came from his Santa Claus-like belly. As Father laughed, he pounded the dining room table; all—laughter, belly, table slaps—came in rhythmic, synchronized motion.

As a child, bearing witness, I always felt a sense of privilege and pride in it all. However, there was nothing special as THAT day. There was nothing that could be better than a celebrity like Rolle being so close and accessible in our personal space.

Mother was always one for pictures. Whether it was birthdays, school plays, family vacations, or hanging out with friends, Mother seemed to always have a camera around, making sure that she captured special moments. Certainly, she was not going to let Esther Rolle get away without proof, so she gathered our family for the photo opportunity. There we were: my mother, Annie Clara White Champion, standing on the second row far left, my father, Rev. George L. Champion, Sr., standing on the second row far right, my oldest brother, George L. Champion, Jr., standing on the front row to the far left, my older sister, Tymy (who was named after my maternal grandmother) Champion, standing on the front row to the far right, and myself, Annie Clara Champion II, the youngest, standing in the middle right in front of Esther Rolle. We were all smiles with teeth except for my brother George who rarely smiled as a kid due to his chipped front tooth. He, too, bubbled with excitement. The picture was taken; our day would end, but the memory would last a lifetime.

The news of her visit traveled fast as friends stopped by the next day in curiosity. Mondays were always a good day. Everyone knew that Monday dinners were leftovers from the huge, delicious meal that Mother prepared the Sunday before, so hungry bellies could expect to be fed.

At the parsonage, when someone was home, our front door was mostly unlocked. People from the church and the Richmond Heights neighborhood would knock, announce themselves and come right on in. George, Tymy, and I hosted many neighborhood peers. We would even play and talk outside with them while chatting about the latest current events, bike riding, and even roller skating. Nearby, the alluring aroma of fried chicken, fried pork chops, fried everything filled the atmosphere, giving us a presupposition of what was going to be on the neighbors' dinner tables.

Some of these youths were members of St. Mark and some were not, but ALL were our friends. Not only would we play with them outside but they would come inside as well to play games or watch television. There was even an older church teenager who would often come by and play the piano that Father bought for Tymy. He was a gifted musician who could play by ear and would often play gospel songs that he heard in church. With his long fingernails tapping on each key and a high tenor voice, he would belt one out if Mother gave him permission, which she often did. The day after Rolle's visit, no one was interested in playing games, watching television, or even hearing the piano.

Everybody wanted to confirm Ms. Rolle's visit. "We heard Esther Rolle was here yesterday!"

"Yep, she was here and we took a picture with her too!" my siblings and I said.

"Wow!" they said in awe.

My paternal grandparents, Rev. George M. Champion and Annie Williams Champion, had to get in on the news as well. Father's parents would often come visit, being that they lived close by in Ft. Pierce, Florida. They were the cutest couple, both sweet, having been married almost 40 years at this point in life. Grandmother was no taller than 4'11". She was dark in complexion with the sweetest smile in the world. Grandfather had pastored local churches in Florida, including the founding of one. He was dearly loved by all who knew him. Just as father had built a new edifice at St. Mark five (5) years earlier, Grandfather had just completed building a new church edifice in Ft. Pierce, Florida.

With a walk similar to the character played by Red Foxx on the hit TV show *Sanford and Son*, Grandfather also had an idiosyncrasy of biting his tongue while listening intently in conversation. As his grandkids, he always greeted us with a big smile and cheer. Before hearing any rap songs from pioneers like Grandmaster Flash and Kurtis Blow, Grandfather's signature rap line was our first and best.

He would always greet us with *"Milk and Water/You must drink plenty/no tea or no coffee/until you are twenty!"*

We would respond with hugs and laughter as he inquired of our status.

After giving us our time, Grandfather would then turn his attention toward Father. "So you think you're big time because Esther Rolle was in your house, huh?!"

There was silence, stare-offs and loud laughs. We were on top of the world and remained this way for awhile.

As the First Family of St. Mark, we were quite busy as we had schedules around church, life, and school. Music was big in our household. George would play the drums while Tymy and I would play the piano. Tymy was very polished, talented, and smart. She always played her favorite, Clementi's *Sonatina in C Major, Opus36,* perfectly. Tymy and I even took up ballet. We were the only African Americans, as well as the largest in size, height and width. Nevertheless, we could still perform a pirouette with the best of them.

Father had a strong personality and never believed in wasting time. He was always busy doing something. By now, he had written many religious books and even had his own cable television show entitled *The Minority Opinion* where he interviewed various local community and political activists on varied subjects of current civic interests. Before leaving the house, he would interrupt our game of Pong, the table tennis sports game that we played on our huge color television, and remind us to watch his TV show as he headed out the door to the television station.

Travel was always big in our house as well. By this time, we had gone on various trips, including a visit and tour of the White House. There was also our first plane ride to Detroit, Michigan for a family reunion. With proper dress, we sat in first class and were treated to a hot breakfast while going and a delicious dinner upon our return. Nothing was casual about us as we flew through the friendly skies.

There were times when my parents would go out of town and leave us with those whom they could trust. This was always important for the First Family of any congregation and for my parents, this was no different. There was a group that Mother and Father could choose from, including my godmother, who would house sit whenever they would go on trips.

* * *

Mother was the facilitating lubricant that kept all schedules on course. She was an 'every woman' as she daily checked homework, did laundry, ran errands, cooked meals, did church work, etc. She was pleasant in nature and very easy to get along with, always offering much grace to any and everybody. As preacher's kids (PKs), we would always have to share things with other PKs who came over to visit on Sundays. There was one particular PK who was always demanding and rude. I despised her ways, not to mention being obligated by my mother to share my toys.

My E-Z Bake oven was my favorite toy and under no circumstances did I want anybody to touch it or my cake mixes. While visiting, I warned her, "You can play with anything else but don't touch the EZ Bake stuff." About a week or so later, I was asleep in my bed when I felt something crawling, and behold it was a couple of ants. I then turned toward the wall to discover a swarm of ants along with packages of my cake mix ripped apart with their contents strewn along the side of the wall. I was livid, while Mother remained calm. As we both cleaned up the mess, I vented my frustration while Mother offered grace, "She doesn't know any better. Forgive and move on."

Mother was easygoing like that most of the time, but then there was a time where I pushed her sweetness to the limit. Speaking of sweets, I loved sweets and often found myself making way to the neighborhood Candy Lady who lived down the street. She had every piece of candy that you can think of: Now and Later, Jolly Ranch, Blow Pops, M&M's, the list goes on and on. While Mother was in the kitchen or elsewhere throughout the house doing chores, I would go in her purse and steal change in order to buy candy. It was three dimes here or two quarters there; whatever change was available in her wallet, I would take it. This stealing thing was something that I had gotten used to because I never got caught.

One day, my stealing habit would follow me in the drug store as I went inside with Mother. While her back was turned, I stuffed my pockets with the loose candy that was near the cash register. The cashier saw me and reported it to Mother. I denied it indignantly, of course, declaring "I didn't take no candy!" as we exited the store. While getting ready to sit down in the car, Mother heard the swish sound of the candy wrappers inside my pocket. My cover-up exposed, she whipped me at the scene of the crime and then took me back in the store to apologize. This stealing episode would be my last as she put the brakes on a future kleptomaniac for good and I never took her kindness for weakness again.

As a lover of current events and history, Mother would archive *NewsWeek*, *Time*, *Ebony*, and *Jet* magazines along with books that she bought from our White House trip about the former first ladies. These publications were neatly organized in a rack that was attached to the bottom of the 19-inch black and white television that was in the master bedroom. As a small child, I would find myself often thumbing through her collection when I saw what appeared to be a familiar face. Excitedly, I ran to tell Mother that I saw Sherman Hemsley from the hit TV show *The Jeffersons* on the cover of a magazine.

Mother looked at the picture and laughed, knowing that her baby girl's worldview was limited primarily because of extensive exposure to black television shows. She preceded to inform me that my mistaken identity of Sherman Hemsley was actually President Anwar Sadat, the President of Egypt. In that moment, she informed me of the historical importance of the peace treaty that he signed with Menachem Begin, the Prime Minister of Israel. The treaty signing had been witnessed by her favorite U.S. President, Jimmy Carter, who had enabled it in difficult negotiations. Mother always took great pride in President Carter because he was from Plains, Georgia, which was only 20 minutes from her hometown of Ellaville, GA. After her teaching moment, she hugged me and said, "One thing's for sure, baby: there is a strong resemblance between Sadat and Hemsley." We both laughed.

Father was a disciplinarian who was serious about education as well. He was also keen on speech. One of his extracurricular activities was being a member of Toastmasters International. Though he was gifted in preaching, he always loved to hone his oratorical skills, seeking to become even better. One day, I travelled with him to a Toastmasters event where he greeted the crowd. Immediately, I noticed that we were the only African Americans in the room. I didn't know how he would fare with speaking to this crowd which was different from our St. Mark Sunday mornings.

Father stood at the microphone and said, "Today, I'm going to speak on the 4 B's. Be Good. Be Strong. Be Brief. Be Gone."

The crowd rumbled with laughter.

Father's charisma prevailed. When it came to public speaking, he took it seriously, so it was of high importance for his children to always pronounce and enunciate words correctly. Whenever we would split a verb, he would always correct us and make us say it three times the correct way. Whenever we got out of line behaviorally, if he wasn't getting the belt, he would put his finger in our face as if it was touching our nose in order to reprimand us. Father was a man who was serious, and didn't take any bad behavior from his children.

Besides being a disciplinarian, Father was also cool, as in the middle of his busy schedule, he would play sports with us, including baseball and basketball. Father would also annually take us and a few of the church and neighborhood youth to Disney World. This was a special treat as we got to ride on Space Mountain, It's A Small World, and see other fun stuff at America's favorite theme park.

However, it was Oct. 1, 1982 which made Father the coolest.

We awoke to what we thought would be a normal school day when Father greeted us and said, "Hey kids, you're not going to school today… you're to get another kind of education."

We anxiously asked, "Where are we going?"

"We're going to EPCOT Center!" he exclaimed as we jumped up and down and ran excitedly around the house.

It was the Grand Opening of EPCOT Center and we would be apart of its history as its first day of thrill seekers. Like Mother, Father was always good with history and making sure that we didn't miss those moments which came once in a lifetime.

Just a year or so earlier, in 1981, he awoke us on a Saturday morning at 5:00 a.m. and said "Wake up! It's time to watch history, kids."

We sat cross-legged in front of our huge colored television in the living room and witnessed Prince Charles and Princess Diana of Wales' wedding from the beginning to the end.

Father always wanted to make sure that we saw historical moments and so that day would be no different in visiting EPCOT. Of course, it was a crowded day that was filled to capacity as what seemed like the whole world would come to see what Walt Disney was up to with this brand new theme park. EPCOT (Experimental Prototype Community of Tomorrow) did what its name says by giving us a glimpse into our future with various attractions including 'Living with the Land,' a boat ride which gave us a tour of greenhouses and spoke about the future growth of fruit and vegetables in a non-traditional manner. We experienced everything that it had to offer from the opening until its closing. Next to Esther Rolle, it was one of our BEST days.

After eating and returning home, George had to keep the party going. Though we were a clergy family steeped in the knowledge of the Bible and lovers of spiritual and gospel music, there were times where we let our hair down and listened to other music as well. George, who was our family DJ, would often turn on the local AM Radio Stations of 1380 WORL or 1600 WOKB to play the latest R & B Music. George was also the one who introduced us to the music of rap artists by being the first in our family to purchase their '45' records or '78' albums. A couple of years earlier, when George brought the Rapper's Delight song by Sugar Hill Gang into our home, my parents asked, "What kind of music is that?"

George schooled them. "It's called RAP Music."

"How long will that kind of music be around?" they asked.

"Forever! Get used to it. Rap is here to stay!" George exclaimed.

The day we went to EPCOT, however, didn't belong to Sugar Hill Gang, instead, it belonged to the hottest band of 1982, The Gap Band, which had an amazing lead vocalist named Charlie Wilson, who belted out their hit single, "You Dropped A Bomb on Me." There was dancing, excitement, and everybody just having a great time. Mother stood in the distance while smiling and shaking her head at the same time.

Father got in on the fun and sang along while to trying to move and sing at the same time.

As he moved, only bending his knees, he would then say, "Good God what is the music doing to me?!"

We laughed and egged him on with our "Go Daddy! Go Daddy!" as he moved in his non-rhythmic fashion.

The Gap Band was prophetic in its music. We just didn't know it yet. The love and cheer that we felt on this PERFECT day would be short-lived due to another kind of bomb that Father would soon drop on us all.

Our FAMILY MATTERS

Whenever there are marital issues, besides the husband and wife, the children are the next to know. Mother and Father were a great team in ministry. They had built a church together, cared for the congregants, community, and engaged Esther Rolle. They even hosted many dignitaries, but conflicts often arose which resulted in arguments that fell on the children's ears. Internally, I was hoping and praying that things would work out between them and somehow they could reconnect in marital bliss. It never happened, and now our family was at a point that I feared the most. One Wednesday, me and my siblings talked amongst ourselves with George leading the pack.

"Did Daddy talk to y'all yet?" George asked.

Tymy responded sadly as she looked down while scratching her head, "Yeah, he talked to me the other day."

I then inquired, "What did Daddy talk to y'all about?"

"Daddy's leaving. He's moving out," George said.

Father had a plan in breaking the news to us. He would take each of us aside to speak of his departure. I was next and I had a hunch it would be soon. A couple of hours later, Father came home and said that he wanted to talk to me alone. We walked up the sidewalk to St. Mark and sat in a room on the side of the sanctuary where only a black leather love seat and chair existed. My heart was beating very fast as I wasn't ready to hear what I already knew he would say. There would be no biblical text or inspirational sermon mentioned here. This time, Father spoke words that would ensue anxiety and fear.

"Baby you know me and your mother have been having problems for a long time."

He said other words but for a moment, I was stuck on his first line.

He then concluded with the words I never wanted to hear. "I'm moving out tonight. We're getting a divorce."

I sobbed.

He consoled me as we took what seemed to be the longest walk home down the sidewalk into the parsonage. Father then gathered everybody in the family room and had prayer. I kept my eyes open for this one. As a matter of fact, I didn't hear Father's prayer. His prayer may have been for God's protection or God's provision. I don't know. My mind was gone. For me, Father should've prayed to keep our family together. At the time, no other prayer made sense to me. Afterwards, he hugged my siblings and I, then proceeded to walk out the door.

My mother gave a final plea, "George, don't leave. Let's get counseling."

I knew what would be his response. He had already made up his mind. I saw it in his eyes.

"Nope. I'm gone Ann," he calmly replied. "I'll be back later to get the rest of my things."

In reflection, I thought of Father's pastoral moments of St. Mark. Father had a special way of bringing people together with his special style of ministry.

He said, "If you've done anybody wrong, go and ask for their forgiveness. If someone in here has blessed you and you never told them, go and tell them, 'Thank you.' This is the time to do it. Go and either ask for their forgiveness or tell them 'Thank you.' Don't worry about others watching. They won't know whether you're saying 'Forgive me' or 'Thank you.' Just move in the Spirit of God!"

My only hope was that the same manner of unity that Father showed in church would be shown at home with Mother. It wasn't. With immense sadness, I watched Father walk down the same hall where we all had posed for the family picture with Esther Rolle. Soon, he was out of the front door with an overnight bag on his shoulder. We all mourned. In a strange way, a funeral occurred that day. However, there was no casket with a dead body or even flowers sitting idly by its side. The only thing that laid in private view were broken hearts and tears of sorrow. Certainly, our family would never be the same and our future was beyond anything we could ever imagine.

The news traveled fast of Father's departure. It made its way into the ears of church members, and the community, leaving most people disappointed and disgruntled over what they had heard. The Bishop over the jurisdiction made a pastoral change. Father was reassigned to a congregation in Tampa, Florida, while the pastor who was at the congregation in Tampa, Florida became the pastor of St. Mark. Things were moving fast, way too fast. We couldn't wrap our minds around it all. To make matters worse, we had to move out of our home. This was really hard for me as it was the only home I had ever known. We had countless Christmases, birthday parties, memories including

Esther Rolle, in that house but this was now our rude awakening, our 'new' reality.

It was our home but it wasn't our house. It was a parsonage, a church house provided for clergy and family, and now we had 30 days to move out so the next clergy family could move in. The trustees, leaders responsible for the church property, would soon enter our personal space, taking inventory of every piece of furniture, China and other things that were brought solely for the parsonage, ensuring that nothing was taken out. There were long, tedious days as Mother would mull over years of accumulated possessions, ensuring that our personal valuables were not mistaken for the church's stuff. It was laborious and grievous to our spirit. Day after day, we would wake up with the harsh reality that our alpha male father was no longer there, no longer in charge of our household.

This was hard for Mother, having been married to Father for fifteen years. Mother was a housewife most of their marriage so her financial dependency was attached to Father. With their marriage being dissolved, she was now our lead. As head of household, Mother was behind the wheel and had to make major decisions—fast.

Mother had now lived in Orlando, FL thirteen years and had created her own friendships. She sought the help of a family friend, a seamstress who did alterations for us throughout the years. Her friend owned a couple of properties around town including a duplex. Fortunately, she was able to make accommodations for us.

The day we left the parsonage, we only had boxes of clothes, and a few personal heirlooms. At one point, when there appeared to be a mix-up of boxes, Mother quickly made things right. "No that doesn't stay here… those go with us."

There were boxes and boxes of photographs that Mother considered precious valuables, especially the one that held the pictures we took with Esther Rolle. From then on, she would keep a close eye on those photograph boxes, making sure nobody got close to them again.

One of the most disheartening things for me was when Mother gave away all of her hats. In seeing Mother wear her hats on Sunday mornings, for it was like seeing a model on a New York fashion runway. Things were now different since she was no longer married to the pastor. Mother's role as First Lady was over, making the hats I loved only a memory.

Some of the church members came to help us relocate to our new home—the Duplex. My godmother would be one of them as she drove us over to our new place in her long blue Chevrolet. Being that we didn't have a car, she offered her vehicle.

"You can use my car anytime, Ms. Champion," Godmother said as she lit her cigarette.

"Thanks Grace. I appreciate it," Mother responded.

There is a saying, "Things can change at a drop of a dime." Well, it seemed like pennies, nickels and quarters were dropping too while the change felt like it was way too much and way too fast.

The duplex was not nearly as plush and lavish as St. Mark's parsonage of course. It was quite the adjustment for four persons to live in a two-bedroom duplex. There would be no celebrity to visit us in this place. Ironically, Esther Rolle fought to have the black father present on *Good Times*, as she deemed it important in the portrayal of the black family. There would no longer be a James Amos character for us. We were experiencing everyday struggles while living out our own version of *Good Times*. The duplex only had two bedrooms, one full bathroom, a kitchenette and a living room. Thankfully, the living room was furnished but we had to furnish our own bedroom furniture, borrowing from a couple of church members. There was no washing machine or dryer so now, for the first time, we had to use a laundromat.

Our first Thanksgiving here would be different from others before. Instead of being the ones to give Thanksgiving baskets to the poor and needy, we were the poor and needy receiving the Thanksgiving baskets. Our fresh and frozen grocery lifestyle was now a mere memory as it had been replaced with canned meats and vegetables. Being new recipients of food stamps and surplus was humbling, and admittedly, the government butter and cheese made the best grilled cheese sandwiches.

Mother kept her head up through it all as she made the best out of a bad situation. We were always calling Mother's name, to which she would usually respond, but when the burdens got too heavy, she would spiritually escape and begin to hum a hymn which was her way of connecting with God. If we called Mother during this time, our request would have to wait. God always came first.

Mother valiantly made the family adjustment as she would daily awake us, cook breakfast, and sometimes have the R&B sounds coming through a small portable radio. One morning, the song "Pass the Dutchie" by Musical Youth was on so we had a family dance moment. We released, if just for a moment, some of the pain from Father being gone from the home.

My parents worked out parental visitation so we would visit Father every other weekend. Our first visit with Father at his new church in Tampa, FL was quite interesting. The church was brown brick. It was very old and traditional unlike St. Mark, which was more contemporary and modern.

The parsonage was quite different as well. It appeared to be a 100-year-old house with 3 levels and carried an old gas oven scent. Father tried to be domesticated and cook in the kitchen only to his travail. The eggs were overcooked and he burnt the toast. The kitchen was Mother's territory and I never saw Father cook anything, not even boil an egg prior to the divorce, so this was a whole new world for him. The endless stairs had a very loud creek that was heard as you walked up each one. You always had to wear socks for if not, you could get a splinter in your foot which was a painful lesson that unfortunately, I learned. The dreary thing about this parsonage was that it was across the street from a cemetery. This was not a good visual for a nine -year-old like myself. After taking a quick shower, I would dress, do a mad dash down the hall into my room, close the curtains and get under the covers with only one eye shut. Scared to death, I would say my prayers and try to get some sleep.

The television sitcom *Family Matters* had a two-parent household living harmoniously under one roof. Across America, in the 1980s, however, this was not the case. The divorce boom was in full effect and we were feeling its vibrations. This transition of now divorced parents was a lot of pressure, especially when it came to packing my weekend suitcase.

One Sunday, while unpacking my things at the parsonage in Tampa, I discovered that I had left my dress at home in Orlando. The only thing that I had in my suitcase was a shirt and a pair of pants. An explanation to Father that I couldn't go to church wouldn't suffice.

He wasn't trying to hear it… "So what you left your dress! Wear your shirt and pants… You're going to church young lady! It's not what's on the outside anyway! It's what's on the inside that matters!" If Father knew my inside, he would've known that I was in pain. If I could turn back time, I would. For me, things were much easier and better back then.

* * *

Employment was something that was quite challenging for Mother. With Father's income now gone, she was now the breadwinner with only crumbs she received as a substitute teacher. Money was tight, but Mother had a survival instinct and knew how to stretch a dollar far and wide. When Mother would go into her reflection of economic struggles and her failed marriage, she would often tell me, "Always keep you a job. Don't ever make the mistake that I made!" When she would say it, she made sure that she had my undivided attention.

After a year or so, Mother earned enough to relocate us to a rental home that was located in the Washington Shores neighborhood of Orlando. The house was located on a street called Bethune Drive, which was named after the African American educator Mary McCloud Bethune, for whom the famous Bethune Cookman University is named. This house was bigger than the duplex we lived in before. It had three (3) bedrooms with 1.5 bathrooms. The .5 bathroom was formerly a closet.

With the economic changes and struggles surrounding us, Mother desired to bring educational stability to her children. Though we were now in our third residential home, I remained at the same local elementary school due to the help of my three elementary school teachers. They had a daily carpool, and somehow Mother got wind of it. Being that they lived near our new home, Mother called and asked if they could pick me up on their route. They obliged.

Mother was resourceful like that, where she would find a way to make things work in order to get a task accomplished. When I was four years old and no longer allowed in Head Start due to a kid fight, Mother made a way and enlisted me in kindergarten early without proof of a birth certificate. She was savvy and didn't mind asking for favors, especially regarding her children.

Another thing that was important to Mother was spiritual stability. Our departure from the parsonage was one thing but our departure from the church building she helped birth with Father was another. Mother made a decision to keep St. Mark as our home church. As the new pastor of St. Mark and his family moved in, there was a mutual respect and understanding between our families. Mother kindly sat further down in the second row, allowing the new First Lady to sit in the assigned First Lady seat that mother established. The new pastoral family was very kind in offering us rides and assistance as well.

My siblings and I remained very active in the church, serving in the Youth Choir and the Young People's Department (YPD), who would constantly instill and enforce the words, "We shall be strong, be brave, be true." This mantra motivated and encouraged us to know that no matter what we face in life, we can overcome it. Music was our precious solace as we would sing and listen to music from gospel recording artists like John P. Kee and New Life as well as the Milton Brunson Thompson Community Choir to help carry us through our wilderness of life.

Outside of spiritual music, we listened and loved the secular music of that day and time. We enjoyed R & B artists such as El DeBarge, Chaka Khan, Prince, and The Jacksons, whom my friends and I salivated over when seeing them in the *Tiger Beat* or *Right On* teen magazines. Our fantasy of seeing them LIVE would come true as St. Mark would carry a bus full of adolescent fans to the Gator Bowl for the Jacksons' Victory Tour Concert.

Though my siblings and I had moments of enjoyment, our dim reality was always before us. Not only did the divorce hit us financially, it also affected us, as the children, emotionally. George was now in high school. It was a hard transition for him as he would get in school fights, one time resulting in a busted lip. Sports were his saving grace, being primarily active in football and track. For the most part, it would keep George centered but that would only last so long. George needed a way out and he found it in Father's sister and brother-in-law who resided in West Palm Beach, FL. They were both disciplinarians and educators who could get George on the right track, escaping the economic and emotional turmoil that plagued us. When

George left to live with them, things were getting stranger by the minute as we witnessed our family circle growing further and further apart.

* * *

Richmond Heights Subdivision would serve as our fourth residential address. We had to move from our Bethune Drive address due to a rodent invasion, which we often heard in the attic as they scurried above our heads. Mother reported it to the "slumlord" but he never tried to correct the problem. Mother took matters in her own hands and moved us to a safe, rodent-free home. Being back in Richmond Heights was a return to our genesis except we were no longer in the "Big House." We were, however, within walking distance from my elementary school, Richmond Heights Elementary School, and St. Mark.

Richmond Heights, a predominately African American subdivision, was built in the 1960s. It's a neighborhood that has streets and parks named after some of the great African Americans legends like Willie Mays, Phillis Wheatley, Crispus Attucks, and Nat King Cole. Our street, Aaron Ave., was named after Hank Aaron, the 'Homerun King' of Major League Baseball who endured challenges and overcame racism, especially when breaking Babe Ruth's homerun record. Our new rental home had three bedrooms, 1.5 bathrooms, with the .5 bathroom being in the main bedroom. There was a small living room that was big enough to hold our borrowed furniture as well as the family piano. Next to the family pictures, the piano was the second most valuable possession. The small dining room merged into the living room with the dining room table being surrounded by mixed folding chairs.

This house would suffice except for one major issue, it had no air conditioning. There was no central air nor an air conditioning window unit. Again, it had no air conditioning. There is nothing more tortuous than living in Orlando, FL with 110 degrees humid temperature and not have an air-conditioned home for heat relief. Friends would stop by for a visit but not too long in fear of passing out due to heat exhaustion. Instead, we would hold company underneath our carport, which had no car. We attempted to cool the house by putting fans in the window only to have the heat blown back in the house, or we would keep our windows open in hopes for some fresh "cool" air, which only happened in the fall and winter seasons. At night, as a cooling method, I would even rub my feet against the metal of the bed, which seemed to be the coldest thing in the house. It often provided some sense of cool relief.

After leaving elementary school, it was time for junior high school. My road would lead to Carver Junior High School, which was named after the great African American scientist, George Washington Carver. It was the same school that my siblings attended and I would follow in their footsteps. Junior high school proved to be exciting as I was in a larger school environment with kids who donned the 'curl,' which felt like an African American hair evolution. It seemed like everybody in the school was styling and profiling the carefree curl, jheri curl, and whatever other kind of curl that required a ton of activator. This was evidenced with what looked like sweat on the backs of many shirts and blouses. Everybody had a 'curl' except me. Mother was conservative, traditional in style, so my consideration of a curl was not an option. Neither were pierced ears.

Years earlier, George and Tymy attended Carver Jr. High School and played in the marching band. George played the drums while Tymy played the b-flat clarinet. Now, I would inherit my sister's clarinet and join the Carver Junior High School Marching Band as well.

We had a great band teacher who was fun with a lovable spirit. He was also a disciplined man who operated in promptness and timeliness. I was usually five minutes late coming to class as he would often warn me yet offer grace. One time, I was caught by the "Surprise Tardy Bell." The consequences were three paddle hits from the principal.

Attempting to slide in after the tardy bell, my band teacher reprimanded me. "Ann Champion, you're going to be late to your own funeral!"

He then sent me to the principal's office for my just punishment.

It would take more than three paddles to reform a chronic late-comer like myself. This would result in a horrible habit that would carry over even in my adulthood. After this incident, I continued to play in the band as we had a great sound with awesome chemistry and dance movements. It was duly noted by others in an invitation and acceptance to perform in one of the Mardi Gras parades in New Orleans, LA.

For me, my band teacher was more like a father figure. One day, during band period, I called him something strange and unusual.

"Daddy," I said in trying to get his attention.

He responded with a, "Huh?"

As I was about to say it again, I self-interrupted as he looked at me strangely in silence. With embarrassment and shame, I realized what I had said. He proceeded with music class as I prayed that none of the other students heard me. Was it a Freudian slip? Maybe so. Besides, Father and I didn't have the best relationship. At this point, I seemed to have removed Father from my mind and replaced him with someone else whom I deemed as a father by my standards.

When it came to Mother's personal life, I was worried. It seemed like the effects of the divorce made her sad. There appeared to be a spark or something missing in her that was there while my parents were married. When we were together as a family, Mother always had a camera or made sure someone around us did. There were plenty of smiles to capture the moment like the one with Esther Rolle but since the divorce, the camera went away and it seemed like we were only left with memories and boxes of pictures that Mother would covet. She would often say that she was holding onto her pictures because they would be worth something one day. Often, I prayed for her happiness and healing. One day my prayers were answered.

While coming home from school, I saw Mother standing in the front yard having a friendly conversation with a gentleman. He was a familiar face. It was a face that I had seen somewhere before. Oh! It was the bus driver. While riding the city bus, I would often see him and Mother engaged in banter. Now, their friendly exchange has gone from the bus to our front yard. He was not at work this day as told by his civilian clothes. Mother had on her usual casual attire which included a sleeveless polyester shirt, pants, and a head band on her thick bob cut hair. She made formal introductions as I went into the house. You can always tell if it's more than casual conversation between a man and a woman just by the body language and gestures. Shortly, after officially meeting the gentleman and going in the house, Mother soon came in afterwards.

She grabbed a light jacket, purse and anxiously announced, "I'm going on a date! I'll be back!" and then walked out the door.

Mother deserved happiness. Father had remarried and moved on with his life, and I desired the same for Mother.

Mother's date with the gentleman soon turned into more dates which eventually would include Tymy and I on a trip to St. Augustine, Florida. We were more than elated to leave our Disney World, Orlando life and take in another side of Florida that we had never experienced. One Saturday morning, we all jumped in the gentleman's deuce and a quarter while heading one hour and half up the road to the nation's oldest city. It was a beautiful day as we walked along the brick paved streets as the weeping willow trees shaded us from the sun. As a teacher, Mother was enamored with seeing the oldest wooden schoolhouse which is a popular museum there. It was a great trip which concluded with good food at a nice restaurant nearby. Mother's suitor was striking all the right chords as he kept a smile on her face as well as ours, showing consistent kindness and hospitality.

Things seemed to be flowing for awhile until one day, I noticed that Mother wasn't talking on the phone as much anymore, nor were there any more date nights. Being inquisitive, I asked her about him as she told me that they were not dating anymore.

Bravely, I then asked two dangerous questions, "Why?" and "What happened?"

Mother never verbally responded. She only offered a stern look as though to say, "I know you're not asking me about my business."

That look with silence immediately prompted me to either immediately change subjects or walk away. Repectfully, I chose the latter as Mother was not the one to discuss her personal adult business, especially with a child. It was never mentioned again.

On a daily basis, I watched the struggles of single parenting as now Mother was working two jobs. She was a substitute teacher by day and a dietary aide at an assisted living facility by night. During the week, Mother would leave home at 7:30 a.m. and then return at 8:45 p.m., making me a "latch door kid." At times, I would find solace at a friend's home or my god sister's house who lived across the street. When Mother returned, we would touch base about our day while seeking to maintain a meticulous home and laundry system. The two jobs paid the bills but most times, it seemed as though it was not enough.

Anxiously, I wanted to help out. One summer, I reached out to a member of St. Mark who was the Director of Housekeeping at one of the largest tourist hotels in Orlando. The hotel was so big that it had two towers that stood next to each other. During the interview, she noticed that my application stated I was only (14) years old and then informed me that I had to be fifteen years old in order to work in the state of Florida. Aware of the situation, I pressed my case. She saw the hurt and tears well in my eyes as I made emphasis to my situation. Somehow, she worked it out and I landed my first job.

The thought that I would be pushing a cart while cleaning others' messes never bothered me because I would get paid for it and be able to help Mother out. When I broke the news to Mother, she listened intently but I couldn't gauge her emotions. Though times were hard, she never wanted me to work. "You know I never wanted you to get a job. Just focus on school," Mother said. "It's only for the summer Mama. Besides, we need the extra money," I responded. After a few minutes of persuasion, Mother consented. Since school was out for the summer, Mother's substitute teacher income would end. "Do they need extra help?" she inquired. "As a matter of fact, they do," I responded.

In the summer of 1988, Mother and I worked together as hotel housekeepers. For Mother, housekeeper work was not foreign. Years earlier, she lived with an aunt for one year while working as a housekeeper in New York City to save for college tuition. Mother was a pro at surviving and was determined that she would teach her daughter the ropes as well. Every summer morning, we would arise, put on our housekeeper uniforms which consisted of a white blouse, dark skirt, name tag, and then head out the door to catch the city bus.

One of my happiest moments was receiving my first paycheck. It was on a Friday. We got paid every Friday, but this Friday would be a special one. In those days, they would allow the housekeepers to play music on the radios in the hotel rooms while cleaning. My song would be the R &B hit "Just Got Paid" by Johnny Kemp. As the radio blared its sound, I was dancing and singing along as I held my first paycheck. It's something about a check made payable to you that declares a sense of independence and freedom. At the age of fourteen, I was feeling this but most importantly, I was able to help Mother out with her needs.

You can never really understand, appreciate or have as much respect for the work that others do until you have done it yourself. Hotel housekeeping can be strenuous work and is often less respected, falling near the bottom of the most desired jobs on the planet. For many years, many women of color would know this plight. This would even be portrayed on television as Esther Rolle played the domestic help on the television series *Maude* before spinning off to *Good Times*.

There was this one time where hotel housekeeping just about broke my spirit. While I was going through my daily work activities, I went into a hotel room for a daily clean. To my dismay, disgust and filth greeted me with feces smeared on the bathroom mirror. The word 'Bitch' was even written with ketchup and mustard on the wall. Alcohol, dirt, and mess were everywhere.

The room was intentionally trashed, not by somebody who could have been intoxicated with alcohol, but with a hateful spirit. The audacity of him, her, or them to do something this awful and then expect somebody else to literally clean up their shit was unfathomable. Angry beyond belief, I ran to get Mother in which we soon reported the crime to the supervisor. When I showed them the scene, they were both apologetic and shared my sentiment. "I'm not cleaning this up!" I told the housekeeping supervisor. She agreed and reported the findings to the Hotel Administration. My housekeeping duties continued that summer and thankfully, I never experienced a room like that one. The memory, however, would remain with me as I vowed to God and myself that I would never work as a hotel housekeeper again.

Soon after that experience, anger for Father reached a climax. The thought of being put in a position to work as a hotel housekeeper due to our harsh economic conditions upset me. Father was now at his fourth church after leaving St. Mark six (6) years earlier. He would come and attempt to take me twice a month on weekends. We would stay overnight at the church parsonage and attend worship on Sunday morning. Most of the times, I would grudgingly go with him while other times, I would refrain.

One Saturday morning, our father/daughter relationship would take a different course. Without even thinking or carefully preparing my words, I verbally let go with my rant. "Why are you so angry with me?!?" Father demandingly said. "I hate you! I hate you!" I declared in response. Feelings of neglect and abandonment spewed toward Father in putting us in this economically deprived situation. This was a big move for me to raise my voice at Father. From the time I opened my eyes in this world, Father put the fear of God in us where we knew the repercussions if we ever disrespected him or stepped out of line. At this point, it didn't matter. It was time that he knew how I felt. Sometimes, when there's tension, one holding back their feelings can do more harm than good.

One should let their truth speak where others cannot just 'hear' the words but 'feel' the words as well. "I'm sorry, baby... I'm sorry..." Father responded as he heard and felt my words. He promised to do better and asked "Will you forgive me?" while hugging me. I responded with a "Yes." Forgiveness began with my father. After that moment, a veil was lifted as I no longer was resentful in going with Father on weekends. Now, I welcomed those times as we began to reconnect and rebuild our status. During this period, I discovered how much I needed him. A dark road lied ahead for me. On this dark road, I would need Father's love and support more than ever.

WHAT'S HAPPENING to us?

The first Friday in June of 1989 served as the last day of my sophomore school year at Jones High School. Jones High was the first public school for African Americans in Orlando. It was formed in 1895 and later named in honor of Professor L.C. Jones, who was instrumental in negotiating the purchase of land for a new site years later. Many African American generations had passed through its halls as well as celebrities including famous actor, Wesley Snipes. Its Music Departments were top-notch with the high-stepping Tiger Pride Marching Band led by a long-time beloved director and educator whom we affectionately called 'Chief,' as well as the concert choir which was renowned in receiving high commendations at the state music competitions.

George and Tymy participated in choir during their tenure at Jones High School. Like a good little sister, I would follow in their footsteps. By now, I had been apart of the concert choir for two (2) years, having reached the status of 'The Master Singers,' which consisted of a select group that was chosen by our beloved choir director. She would refer to the choir members as her "sugarlumps." Mrs. Hargrett was more like a school mother who always kept cold medicines for sickness and deodorant for good hygiene than a teacher. She was a no-nonsense, disciplined, perfectionist preacher's wife who made sure that we pronounced and enunciated every syllable of each song. As a lover of the negro spirituals and the classicals, it was required that we memorize each chorus from George F. Handel's "Messiah," which we performed before hundreds every year.

This year as with every year, the choir was set to sing at our high school graduation which was always on a Saturday, the day after the last day of school. On this Friday, we had practiced quite a few pieces from our repertoire including the Sound of Music classic "Climb Ev'ry Mountain" and the Negro spiritual, "Soonah will be Done." After leaving school, while walking home from the bus stop, I remember having this strange feeling again. It was a feeling that I had experienced more recently in that someone was watching me and it wasn't just God.

When I got home, I spoke with Mother, ate dinner, took a shower, talked on the phone, and prepared my choir attire. Eventually, I would fall into a deep sleep only to be awaken by a real life nightmare. Suddenly, I felt a gloved hand masked over my mouth. There was a smell of musk and alcohol that wreaked in the atmosphere, along with a strange male voice who had an accent. A knife was then put to my throat as the criminal told me if I screamed, he would cut my throat. My hands were then tied behind my back as he stuffed my mouth with what felt like some sort of material. My heart pounded fast as I was in a trance due to the tragedy that was taking place to me—my 15-year-old body. When the madman left, my half naked body lay in a pool of sweat, liquids, and musk as my body shook in disbelief. When I figured he was gone, I ran into my mother's room crying and screaming that I had been raped.

Mother awoke shocked with her mouth open as we both screamed and hollered. Once she managed to gather herself, she called the police and found clothing to cover me. While waiting, we feverishly looked to see how he got in and there it was, he came through the back door. When the authorities arrived, they asked a plethora of questions as they retrieved evidence, including the seat of the chair where I recently sat. Father soon arrived and hugged me tight as he proceeded to speak with authorities about the situation. They then informed me and my parents that they would have to take me to the hospital for an Emergency Contraceptive and Rape Kit which is otherwise known as a sexual assault forensic exam. It is used to obtain DNA evidence. Eagerly, I then asked if I could shower and change clothes before we left, but they said that I couldn't due to DNA that needed to be obtained. Soon after, I was referred to a rape advocate who wore a pantsuit and had curly blonde hair. She was very supportive and comforting in my grief.

When we walked outside, I was greeted by a crowd of curious, concerned neighbors and onlookers. There was also the sight of multiple police as all appeared to look at me startled and amazed. Disheveled I was with my hair sticking straight up in the air, torn pajama shirt, and cut off pants that Mother gave me for decency in order to cover up my ripped underwear. The short walk from our front door to the back of the police car felt like forever as the world witnessed my brokenness. The predator left nameless with no one ever seeing or knowing him while I was renamed shame being exposed with all of his residue. Rattled and anxious are the words that best describe my emotions as we made our way to the hospital for the necessary procedures. My parents later joined me and continued to offer consolation and support.

My biggest relief came in coming home and being able to take a shower after hours of the horrible stench and bodily liquids that laid upon me. When I got in the shower, I scrubbed repeatedly and abrasively from head to toe in trying to remove every cinch of the thief/rapist from me. After thirty minutes, Mother knocked on the door to inquire of my status and I told her to give me more time. After (30) more minutes, she said gently it was time for me to get out of the shower. She and Father then revealed that I was to go live with Father in Jacksonville for the summer to escape the pain and anguish as caused by the serial rapist. Father lived between two residences. One in Orlando where he lived with my stepmother and the other in Jacksonville which served as the parsonage of the church he pastored. Soon, I packed my things, hugged Mother, then I drove away with Father in his Lincoln Continental Town Car.

Father's car was his everything as he would drive it on the Florida freeways between his permanent residential home in Orlando and the churches where he was assigned. His first Lincoln, to my recollection, was a white one then it was a forest green one, a burgundy one, and now a blue one. He always said that he was a "Lincoln Man" and for him, there was no better quality car. A ride in his Lincoln was more than just a ride—it was always an experience. Being that he wasn't a smoker, Father would keep Coffee Nips or Freedent gum in his ash tray and was always quick to share.

Under normal circumstances, the car would be filled with conversation including banter and laughter, but this tragedy caused a shift. There was a silence and a distance in trying to wrap our heads around what just happened.

As Father drove, I stared out the car window with despair and emptiness. Father said, "We need to forgive him."

As I turned my body toward him and looked with a strange stare, he barely managed to look in my eyes.

He soon hit the dashboard and declared, "I want to kill him for what he did to you but we got to forgive him, baby!" He returned to *his* forgiveness.

Father's anger toward the rapist appeared more authentic than his learned theological one. At first, it felt like he was repeating the corporate Sunday School phrase that we were all taught to say as if there was something wrong with being angry or that God would be upset if we didn't quickly forgive. So often, the initial focus is to quickly forgive the transgressors while the victims delay processing their own pain which could lead to devastating effects on one's self-worth, and livelihood. I wasn't about to do that.

In the console of his car, Father kept quite a repertoire of cassette tapes that included gospel artists such as James Cleveland, New Jersey Gospel Choir, Florida Mass Choir, as well as artists like Lou Rawls, Richard Pryor, and even Neil Diamond, which oddly stuck out like a sore thumb. In an earlier time, I asked him about it and he said he liked Neil because his songs had great stories. "Though he's jewish and I'm black, I still connect with him. It's with our stories where we connect with people," Father said.

He also had preaching cassette tapes. A great preacher always loves to listen to other great preachers besides themselves. Father had a good friend who pastored one of the largest Baptist churches in Ft. Lauderdale, FL. He would put his cassette tape in for consolation. After seeing that the preached word was doing more for him than it was for me, he then turned to me and offered music that would heal my wounded spirit. "I bought this new music from the store last week," he said. It was the new *Heaven* cassette tape by BeBe and CeCe Winans. Every song would minister to my pain especially "Like a Bridge Over Troubled Waters." While continuing to stare out the car window, I closed my eyes and let the sounds of BeBe and CeCe soothe my soul—soothe my soul.

When we pulled in the driveway of the Jacksonville church parsonage, Father told me that Tymy would be staying with us. It had been a while since I last saw Tymy. After her junior year at Jones High School where she was on the National Honor Society, Tymy left Orlando and went to live with our paternal grandparents in South Florida. After awhile, she moved with our aunt, a registered nurse living in Miami, FL. It was in Miami where Tymy would graduate from high school and then attend a community college. At this point, she was now staying in Jacksonville with Father. When I walked in the house, she was seated on the ledge of the fireplace. We greeted and hugged as she offered her sympathies. "I'm sorry about what happened to you," she said in a child-like voice. As she expressed her sentiments, her look gazed off in the opposite direction while I stood grateful that she wasn't there.

There was also another gentleman who was there. We exchanged greetings as he left the house, clearly on his way somewhere very important. He was older, in his thirties, intelligent, respectful, and very kind. When inquiring of his status, Father informed me that he was a recovering drug addict. His mother was a pastor at a nearby church and had asked Father to serve as a mentor for him. 'Brett' was temporarily living at the parsonage until he was able to get back on his feet. For me, this guy didn't meet the usual neighborhood crackhead profile that consisted of missing teeth, tattered clothing, scrawny with big 'wiry' eyes. Instead, he was quite the opposite.

"What's his story?... What happened?" I asked.

Father began to explain. "At one point in his life he was doing quite well for himself as an upper middle-class African American. He was successful in that he was married and worked in a corporative executive position. He began to experiment with drugs, and then one thing led to another."

Again, not your typical "crackhead," at least the ones that I had seen on the streets of Orlando.

Father then blurted out, "That sh** is destroying our Black men! I'm trying to do something about it!"

By helping Brett, Father was doing his part. As we talked, the television blared the theme Good Times in demanding our attention. We didn't think twice about it.

That night, while lying in bed, I tossed and turned with terror memories from the night before. Soon, I found myself in Father's room standing at his bedside when I turned on his nightstand lamp.

Startled by my presence, Father sat up on the side of the bed, put on his glasses and inquired, "What's wrong baby?"

"I'm not ready to forgive him," I said with tears coming down my face.

"I know," he said. "I know." Father hugged me and afterwards, offered no more words. It was what I needed the most.

In the following days, Father would take me with him everywhere. Soon, I discovered that Brett wasn't the only man Father helped. Father sat on a Board of the Drug Rehabilitation Program and would often speak and mentor other African American Men who struggled with this addiction. In those meetings, I sat off in observation and listened to the men share their stories. Our calendar would also include sick and shut in visitations and community clergy meetings. In his down time, Father even offered a few driving lessons on the church parking lot being that I was of age to receive my restricted driving license.

We would often find solace in fast food while playfully arguing over which restaurant had the best fries. Fried chicken, however, was our thing and whenever we were out and about, Father would call the church secretary to see if she wanted lunch. Always in agreement, she would thankfully say yes!

One day, while returning to the church with lunch, Father overheard the secretary's conversation in what would appear to be sharing of church business. As we approached her office, Father looked at me and motioned the "talk too much" hand sign. When entering her office, she was surprised as she almost jumped out of her chair, abruptly hanging up the phone.

Father would soon give his one-liner, "What's the root word of secretary?"

She looked puzzled as to why he was asking her the question.

Father then said, "SECRET… Shhhhhhhh," while putting his index finger over his mouth.

In response, I chuckled as Father had this comedic edge in getting his point across. We delivered her lunch and then headed back to his office.

Things seemed to be going smoothly for the most part as we were trying to readily adjust and reset from that horrible day in June. Later that summer, George would soon pay a visit. He greeted everyone with his signature greeting, "HEY HEY HEY… G 3 in the house," as he offered bear hugs and kisses with his strong, muscular frame. We then introduced him to Brett who was on his way out the door to his drug rehab program.

After Brett left, George was very attentive and serious as he inquired of my status, all the while being very curious of our houseguest.

"So who is this brother that is staying here?" George asked.

We explained his situation, including the fact that he was recovering from drugs.

"So y'all got a crackhead living up in here? Is that what y'all saying?"

We never looked at Brett as a "crackhead." He was just a brother that took a wrong turn and so far, as Father and myself were concerned, Brett had proven himself to be very well-mannered and kind so we adamantly defended him in speaking highly of his demeanor and character.

George wouldn't buy it. He said, "No, no… Y'all crazy to believe that he is clean and won't go back on crack… like they say 'One time is too many and too many times is not enough!' Once a crackhead… Always a crackhead!"

Father rose up and vehemently rejected that notion. "That's a lie! People can change! I don't believe that for one minute about him! Brett's going to be alright, just watch!"

So far, Father was right. Brett was doing everything *right*. We were really enjoying Brett's company and it looked like his life was headed in the right direction until ONE DAY, Brett didn't come home as usual. His life was set according to a schedule. We all knew his schedule and he knew ours. Dinner was cooked and we sat around waiting for him to walk through the door. Thirty minutes had passed and then an hour went by. Father called his drug counselor who said that Brett didn't show up for his meeting that day. Father then called the director of the program who after research and investigation, reported back that no one had seen Brett as well.

We all got nervous and anxious trying not to think the worse. With little conversation, we ate dinner as Father's concern and anxiety grew. We knew exactly what he was thinking because we were all thinking it, too. After a few hours, Brett finally walked in the door. His eyes were red and his smile seemed fraudulent as he nervously greeted everyone. As he stood in the living room, a strange burnt odor wreaked from his brown corduroy blazer. It was an odd smell that I had never experienced and yet will never forget. Apparently, he had relapsed. Father got up from his recliner and said to him, "Let me see you in my office." They went in.

It made no sense for Father to close the door in trying to be discreet for he, as all of us Champions, were naturally loud talkers. Father wasn't holding anything back in his words. Metaphorically speaking, his clergy collar came off as he spewed a series of expletives that were enough to make a mouth drop and a head turn. After Father concluded, he exclaimed, "Get the hell out!" Brett left and we sat in the living room, with feelings of disbelief and sadness. Father, Tymy, and I were sadly surprised but not George. George sat calmly with a smirk on his face because his initial suspicion was correct. He knew all along how this story would end as he leaned over and whispered in my ear, "Told you… once a crackhead, always a crackhead."

Hurt and disappointed more so than all of us was Father, as he took a chance on a man who could not resist the urge of crack cocaine and a result, his family was endangered. This is when I learned that ministry can be risky. You can invest in people with great hopes that they will overcome or even succeed in a particular endeavor but in their humanity, they can fall short and let you down just like Brett did.

The summer soon ended and it was time for me to return home to Orlando. As we drove up to the house, the change was blatant as Mom had black 'jail like' bars on the outside of the windows. In walking inside, I immediately noticed that the once rickety wooden back door where the criminal entered was replaced with a steel one. My hometown was still Orlando but my home was now Ft. Knox as my parents put it on lockdown to not only keep other intruders out but to keep me safe within. Father walked me in and then said, "I'll be checking on you. You hang in there baby… Alright. Love you." We hugged and he left.

Mother shadowed me to my bedroom where the crime had occurred. "I got you a new bed," Mother said. The bed was replaced but the memory was not removed as I stood there for a few seconds while the rape replayed in my thoughts. I then self-interrupted and began to talk to Mother and catch up on things that I missed over the summer.

"People have been calling and asking about you in church. They said that you were in their prayers," she said.

While shaking my head up and down, I offered no words in response.

Mother continued. "You know your girls have been calling non-stop and I told them that you were coming home today so they will probably be here…"

Just as soon as she said it, I heard the car and tire marks skid in the driveway as car doors began to slam and feet shuffled quickly to the door. The sound of door knocking and bell ringing seemed to come at once. They had arrived. My best friends were here. Jones High School and choir sealed our sacred bond. We were preacher's and church deacon's daughters who were "good girls," which made for a special blend of mischief and wit.

Mother went to her room giving me time with my besties. When I opened the door, they blurted my name, covered me with hugs and riddled me with sarcasm like only they could do.

"We have been calling all summer and have not been able to reach you! Annie C (how they referred to my mom when she was not around) and Pierre (nickname they gave to my father because he always donned a beret with his suits) have kept us in the dark. What is going on? Are you alright?"

As they continued talking, offering cares and concerns, I mentally went somewhere.

We were best friends, free and open to talk about any and everything. Like the television sitcom, *What's Happening!* we were the female version of the characters played by Fred Barry, Ernest Lee Thomas, and Haywood Nelson whose conversation and encounters would be full of school talk, neighborhood gossip, and boys. Our time was well spent at the nearest fried chicken joint where we would order a family size chicken meal with fries, corn on the cob, biscuits, and apple pies. In an attempt to ease our health guilt, we would order five (5) cups of large water instead of soda as though the water could wash away the 10,000 calories we had just devoured. We were close but I was not ready to go into the depths of the rape. At the time, it was just too painful. As I leaned on the metal folding chair which was out of place with the other chairs at our dining room table, my emotion was heavy with no tears or words. They sensed it and offered words of affirmation through a group hug.

* * *

In the fall of that year, I would return to Jones High School as a junior. On the first day of school, I was nervous as my parents would sense my anxiety. In response, Father would drop me off at school. When pulling up on the school grounds, the anticipation was high among the other students as they offered "daps," hugs, laughter in catching up on their summer escapades. My summer, however, was quite different from theirs. As Father pulled in and parked the car, we both got out.

He inquired hesitantly, "Do you want me to…?"

Emphatically, I shook my head signaling the word 'no.'

For me, no matter how painful the rape, I could not have Father *protecting* me by walking me to class on my first day back to school.

Father sensed that so he walked over to me and said, "If you can make it through this, you can make it through anything!"

There would be many other challenges to face in life. I would have to get through this one first. Father was determined that I would.

He then offered prayer and afterwards, he said, "Look at me, eyeball to eyeball." Father would always say that to my siblings and me when he demanded our undivided attention.

"You will get through this. Hear me... You will get through this... Hold your head up... shoulders back. You're a Champion... remember that!"

It felt like I was in a boxing match now standing in the corner with Father as my trainer offering motivation before the fight. My opponent would be the court of public opinion as I would soon weigh in on supposed whispers. The school bell rang and it was time for me to go inside but what lied ahead within those school walls would soon be determined. Internally, prayers continued for God's strength to carry me through it.

Out of personal tragedy, even if it's known to others, people will respond to you based off your behavior. If you seem 'alright,' they won't bother you with profuse questions or concerns. When entering the school halls, I was alright in speaking to friends and classmates. My best friends more than ever helped me in my adjustment. They always made things better with their wit, humor and candor. Everything seemed to be going fine and things were returning to normalcy but as I was attempting to put that awful night in June out of my head, someone would bring it back to my memory.

There was a young man there who had shown interest. We were in the 'talking' phase where you're not dating but just getting to know each other.

One day, as he was walking me to class, he said, "I heard something about you today!"

My heart fluttered. Instinctively, I knew where he was going before he said it. "What did you hear?" I asked.

"I heard you was raped!" It was the way he said it.

It wasn't caring or comforting. His expression was a look of disgust not for the perpetrator but for me. It appeared as though he was second-guessing why he showed interest.

I responded, "You can't believe everything you hear."

People were talking. He confirmed it. It left me feeling like I was in Nathaniel Hawthorne's novel, *The Scarlet Letter*, but instead of being publicly humiliated by wearing an 'A' for adulteress as shown on the character's chest, I was privately shamed in wearing an 'R' for raped that was carried in my heart. Feelings of disenchantment were aimed toward him for carrying the bone of the crime. Needless to say, our conversation would soon end along with my interest.

One would have thought that with the tragedy of a rape, and the witness to a crack relapse, things couldn't get worse, but they did. Later on that year, Father was involved in a fatal car accident that nearly took his life due to his narcolepsy. Father also had to relocate once again to another church in another

city. Just to think, a decade earlier, we were all riding high in
Orlando as we celebrated the company of the celebrity, Esther
Rolle. Now, we had all sank low as life's twists and turns seemed
to have us ALL in a dismal place.

On Dec. 31, 1989, the last day of the year, I went to St.
Mark for Watchnight Service, which is a late-night service on
New Year's Eve that provides Christians the opportunity to
reflect on the year that passed and pray for the year that is to
come. The church was packed with people and the worship
service was high in the spirit of God. For the last ten minutes
of the service, we knelt in prayer at the pews as I called on God.
The pastor counted down each last remaining minute of this
dreadful year with each 'watchman' giving the specific time.
As the clock hit midnight, the congregation rejoiced like crazy.
My praise was in advance carrying hope and prayers that the
upcoming year would be much better than the previous one.

It's a DIFFERENT WORLD

God answers prayers. The last two (2) years of my high school career were wonderful. In continuing to be active in school activities, I dated a couple of suitors, even attended the prom with a respectful young man who didn't know of my past or at least didn't make mention of it. For fun, I even got into a little mischief with my class by participating in a "skip party" that was held in Jones High Auditorium. Thankfully, the repercussions weren't that severe. After seven (7) years of depending on public transportation and hitched rides, which I detested, we finally got our own car. It was a burgundy 1986 Buick Century Limited which couldn't come at a more perfect time, being that I had just received my driver's license. We even got an air conditioning unit that was fixed in the front window which made for a sweet homegoing. For Jones High Homecoming Festivities, I was "Miss Choir," and set to graduate in 1991 while maintaining an honor roll GPA.

College was next on the agenda and attending a Historically Black College or University (HBCU) was my main priority. As fans of the television show *A Different World*, myself and thousands of African Americans watched faithfully to see what drama would take place at the predominately black college. Its influence was felt as the enrollment in HBCU's skyrocketed across the country during the years that it aired. Most of my classmates were in search of their own *Different World* experiences which included Florida A & M University (FAMU), Tallahassee, FL, North Carolina AT&T, and more.

My inner circle had other interests. Two of us chose Tuskegee University, Tuskegee, AL, while another picked Bethune Cookman University, Daytona Beach, FL. My choice would be Clark Atlanta University, Atlanta, GA.

My parents were on board with my decision to attend an HBCU. It was 'in the blood' as my grandmother Champion graduated from Bethune Cookman Institute (the name before Bethune Cookman College or University) in the 1930s with a teaching degree. Father graduated from Edward Waters College (the name before Edward Waters University), Jacksonville, FL while Mother graduated from Ft. Valley State College, Ft. Valley, GA. Even a few years earlier, my parents supported George's decision to attend Morris Brown College, Atlanta, GA. My parents knew I loved Atlanta so my choice of Clark Atlanta University was of no surprise to them.

Around this time, Mother and I were experiencing our share of disagreements. As a senior in high school, I had the "grown woman" syndrome in thinking that I knew everything. Mother would quickly remind me that I didn't. Her complexion was also getting darker as her skin shade went from a pecan tan to a dark brown. Now sweating more profusely, Mother's temper gauge was getting shorter. Later, I discovered she was going through menopause. When August arrived, I was all set, packed up, and ready to go except for this feeling of leaving Mother. Even with our spats, and mother/daughter challenges, something inside of me didn't want to leave her—alone.

One day, Mother was sitting in her room, on the edge of her bed, wearing her moo-moo while leaning down with elbows on her lap. She was watching television on her small colored tv which sat on her dresser surrounded by organized baskets of bills and other important papers. Soon, I sat next to her, looked at her, and took her hand. As she moved her eyes from the television to my own, she sensed my feelings like only a mother can.

"What's wrong?" Mother asked as I just looked at her silently.

She continued, "You're worried about me. Don't worry about me. I'll be alright. You need to go... get out of this neighborhood... don't even think about staying around here... LIVE your LIFE... That's what you need to do for me... Live YOUR life!" We hugged and then stared at the television together.

It was a beautiful day in August when we traveled to Clark Atlanta University. Mother was nostalgic in speaking about her Ft. Valley State College days during our seven-hour road trip to Atlanta. As we drove up I-75-85 North and rode through Atlanta, we were greeted, as earlier times before, with the most beautiful skyline ever. As a small child, I loved visiting relatives who lived there. There are fond memories with my favorite cousin whom I shared laughs and walks from her home on Heather Drive to Greenbrier Mall for a look at the latest fashions and the cutest boys. During those times, I made a declaration that one day, I would move there and live forever.

It was something special about this city where just breathing in the air meant a better life, times, pride, and success, especially for black people. Clark Atlanta University would be my pathway to getting a whiff. It was the school to notable alumni such as James Weldon Johnson who wrote the National Negro

Anthem, "Lift Ev'ry Voice and Sing" and Emmanuel Lewis who starred in the hit television Show *Webster*. As we drove on the campus, students and parents were everywhere in trying to get adjusted and settled to our new life—new world.

Clark Atlanta University, whose motto is "I'll Find A Way or Make One," had four dorms on the main campus with three being girl dorms and one being a boy dorm. My dorm room assignment was Pfeiffer Hall, Room 302. Pfeiffer Hall was one of the oldest dorms on campus which meant no elevators. It was challenging carrying trunks of stuff up three levels but we did it. Along with no elevators, there also wasn't any air conditioning. Students expressed many grievances and complaints about this non-amenity but for me and my history with no air conditioning, I could easily make the adjustment.

When we arrived at our room, we were taken by the size. It seemed as though they assigned my roommate (which was one of my best friends) and me a 'matchbox' being the smallest room in the dorm. With the dorm being full to capacity and every freshman already receiving their room assignments, we were stuck, so we used our creativity in making the best out of what we had. Immediately, we converted our twin beds into bunk beds and arranged our belongings so we could have some walking space.

Our room faced the main courtyard with a beautiful old maple tree standing in our view. As we lifted up the window to look down, the sight looked familiar as we swore that we were looking at a scene from Spike Lee's, *School Daze*. We jokingly imitated actor Laurence Fishbourne's character when he called up to actress Kyme's character, and hollered "Yo Rachel!" in trying to win back her affection.

Dorm life was quite diverse being much different from my Orlando lifestyle that often dealt me the sameness. It was composed of a melting pot of young black women from all around America with different backgrounds and experiences. We shared a community bathroom with some being more modest in their bath wardrobe while others shamelessly wore a t-shirt, panties, and a pair of flip flops whose sound reverberated through the halls.

In meeting other students, I enjoyed listening to their stories and distinct accents from Racine, Wisconsin; Bronx, New York; Los Angeles, CA; and Oklahoma City, Oklahoma whose accent was most unusual in its twang sound. Their fashion style was different in that New Yorkers wore baggy clothes and those from LA sported t-shirts (usually white), cut off-shorts, and Burkenstocks (Burks), with socks, while others had on shorts, sandals, jeans, and baseball caps.

Initially, I had a more formal wardrobe in assuming that business casual was the attire for most college students in Atlanta. During one of our mother/daughter spats, Mother tried to warn me that I didn't need to take so many dresses and pantsuits.

"Those kids are going to dress casual. They don't wear those kind of clothes in college!" she said.

Believing she was wrong but now seeing that she was right, I had to make my way to the neighborhood clothing store for a new wardrobe.

It seemed as though there was always activity, loudness in Pfeiffer Hall. At times, when we were homesick, we would party and play our music to represent our state. We would gather in the halls and jeer as each group danced to their home music. Those from Louisiana, would party to DJ Jimi "Where They At?" while New Yorkers would play Crystal Waters, "Gypsy Woman," West Coast would party to DJ Quik, "Tonite," Texans would groove to Geto Boys' "Mind Playing Tricks on Me," and then when it came to "Florida Music," my music, me and the rest of the Floridians would get hyped as we joined in gyration to 2 Live Crew, "I Wanna Rock/Doo Doo Brown."

In the midst of our music diversity, we shared one song of beautiful harmony by the R&B Group, Jodeci "Forever My Lady." With hands raised high and eyes closed, we belted out the lyrics like we were in church testifying to our feelings. It was feelings of high school boyfriends left behind with sights set on intimate prospects that we were soon to get. There were fun and crazy times in Pfeiffer Hall and I was more excited in being chosen to represent them in Clark Atlanta's Homecoming Court.

We enjoyed college life outside of Pfeiffer Hall as well. There were always parties on and off campus. As freshmen, we received three warnings from others, especially when it came to alcohol. First, we were told to beware of our surroundings and always BYOB, which stood for bringing your own bottle of alcohol. In doing so, one will know it's a safe drink. The second warning was to never leave your drink unattended. The last was to limit your input of a potent mix of cherry kool-aid and vodka, which was the name given to one of the fraternity's signature party drinks. This last warning was essential because the cherry

Kool-Aid would overpower the vodka in making you think that the vodka was absent from the drink. If too much was consumed, you could wake up the next morning in a strange place next to a strange person and wonder "How did I get here?" These things were kept in mind while I responsibly got my groove on.

Because freshmen weren't allowed to have cars on campus, we did everything by walking or catching the MARTA public transportation. We would often take walking trips to the West End Mall to get our nails done and to refill on personal supplies. This trip would always include male harassers who would honk their horns and express their attraction out of car windows while driving down the street. Along with our class attendance and study, this was just a part of our college life that came with new experiences and even risky propositions.

One day, a dorm friend from Brooklyn inquired of our interest in a group date. "Hey y'all! I just met a group of guys from Detroit at the mall. They were really cool, ballers, but cool. They asked if I had friends and if so, they would like to take us out all for dinner and just share some good times together... No strings attached." We looked at each other as my eyebrow raised in suspicion, thinking "good times" was not the same kind of *Good Times* that Esther Rolle and other cast members gave us on television. It was something else attached to this date.

My friend continued to stake her claim like a used car salesman with a fast-talking New York accent style in reassuring us that these guys will not want anything from us but a good dinner and good company.

"Just trust me girls… I have a good read on people. Now they are 'ballers' but they're cool people. Let's just go and have a good meal… for FREE."

She said the magic words… *Good Meal* and *Free.*

In college, cafeteria food can get old really quick, as it was decent but tasted nothing like 'Mama's cooking'. As college students being tied to a strict budget, our dinner would either be a bowl of Ramen Noodles or a wing on wheat from the family grocery story that was located near the campus. We said 'Yes' as five of us readied ourselves to look nice for our blind 'baller' dates.

When they arrived, our five randomly paired with their five as each gave an alias to ensure no trolling took place once our encounter was over. We then rode over to a 5-star restaurant on Peachtree in a black Cadillac Escalade. During the ride, we engaged in small talk with our individual dates as well as the group. Cool and calm on the outside but nervous on the inside, I was not fully convinced that these guys just wanted good food and company.

After the 'ballers' inquired of our background, and college status, one of my friends asked, "So what do you guys do?"

There was a frozen silence and smiles as most thought, "That's a stupid question. You know what they do so why are you asking?"

One of the 'ballers' responded to the awkward moment by confirming what we already knew.

"What do we do?" he asked as he finished swallowing the last bite of filet mignon on his plate.

"We're pharmaceutical representatives!" he exclaimed.

We all tumbled with laughter.

After dinner, they asked if we were interested in hanging out longer and we respectfully declined. Internally, I was growing more anxious by the minute. No peace would come until we arrived back on campus safe and sound.

As the Escalade pulled up on the campus, the driver asked again. "Are y'all sure y'all don't want to hang out longer?"

As he said it, he pulled out what looked to be a prescription bottle and began to pour white powder onto a mirror that he had beside his seat. This was totally out of my league. My only knowledge of it was seeing Al Pacino's character snort it on the movie *Scarface*. The actual sight of it up close and personal was on another level.

"No. We're good… we're good," I told the driver while my friends were getting out of the car, though not quick enough for me.

In reality, I subtly moved them along but in my imagination, I was screaming "Hurry up and get the hell out!" Once we were free of their presence, the car door closed behind us as we all breathed a sigh of relief knowing that our encounter could have taken a bad turn. They say, "God takes care of babies and fools." Fools we were in making that bad blind date decision. For all of us, it was a lesson well learned.

Panty Raids were something that was popular on college campuses everywhere. Mother talked about it when reminiscing about her college days in the late 1950s. It's where a group of male students would sneak into a women's dormitory with the objective of stealing panties. At this point, the two other female dorms had been attacked by guys from the only male dorm on campus and that night, it was rumored that Pfeiffer Hall would be their next target as spoken in our dorm meeting.

Our dorm president addressed us and encouraged us to take action. "They're coming with their masks, water guns, and God knows what else. We have to be ready, so mount up, sistahs!"

There were loud cheers in response.

The sun soon set and the moon rose. We were on watch when all of a sudden, masked men in black ran through our doors with water guns trying to make their way to our dresser drawers for our draws. We fought them off with our heavy water gun artillery, pillows, and clawed our way through with loud sounds and physical force, demanding that they get out. It was horseplay at its finest as we all got gushed in the eye with water in trying to fight them off. We were able to fend off a few but then others broke through and grabbed their winning prize, our panties, as they flaunted them in our face running out of our building. When the raid finished, we were all exhausted, tired as we looked around at the dusk of mess that surrounded us. There were torn pillows with fallen feathers everywhere, but a fatigued fight with a foe of freshmen boys would prove nothing compared to another kind of fight that was lurking in the shadows.

April 29, 1992 is the day that I awoke from a crazy night of trying to literally save my panties. It appeared that things would be a normal day until someone hollered through the halls "They let those m****f***ers off!" It was the Rodney King Trial. The jury had just acquitted three of the officers who on video used excessive force in beating a Los Angeles black man,

Rodney King. The talk was spreading rapidly around campus and the more we heard it, the more upset we felt. Groups started galvanizing and organizing non-violent protest rallys. The next day, plans went into action as my roommate and I decided to join them with our chant and fists raised high: "NO JUSTICE… NO PEACE." Students were marching from all around the city but somehow in the midst of our protests, neighborhood looters came alongside us creating madness and mayhem.

The riot had begun and government officials were not going to stand by with this civil unrest. While we marched, tear gas was thrown into the crowds, consuming us, halting us, and leaving us with a horrid eye-burning sensation. We pressed on and continued in our protests. Upon returning to campus, our dorm was evacuated due to the protests so we found refuge at a friend's place until we were allowed back in. It was the longest day ever. Being that it came on the week of finals, it made for an even longer week.

Early the next morning, I received a phone call from a familiar voice, "She who hoots with the owls by night cannot soar with the eagles in the morning!" It was Father in dramatic fashion offering his morning greeting.

"I've been watching the news young lady! Things not looking good up there!" he said.

In response, I expressed my grievance about the Rodney King verdict and why it was important for us to non-violently protest.

Father responded, "Yeah, that's important, but your finals are too. That's why I need you to study hard, be safe and do well. I'll be there next Sat. to pick you up."

After completing my freshman year, I returned home to Orlando where I took on a job, revisited my besties, and counted the days to return to the city I loved most. My sophomore year moved me to Bumstead Hall which was located off the main campus on James P. Brawley St. It was one of newer dorms that thankfully had air conditioning.

One day, I received a phone call from Mother that would emotionally take me to that daunting day in June of 1989. Initially, we had lighthearted conversation and then she moved into the more serious nature.

"The investigator called me today. There's a court case coming up for the guy who did it." Mother was hesitant in relaying the information, almost as if she didn't know what my reaction would be.

"That's good. I'm glad they caught him," I said with a faint voice.

There were no questions or inquiries on my part. Early on, I had decided that energy and time would be used on myself. My focus would be on my survival through faith, education, and other positive means. If I put all of my energy on the who's, why's and whereabouts of the rapist then he would take from me more than he already had. I wasn't going to give him that satisfaction. This was the first time Mother and I ever discussed 'him' and it would be our last.

Time moves fast when you're in college. My junior year would be full of studies, an expansion of my friendship circle as well as an outdoor college party called "Freaknik." This major event attracted thousands of African Americans everywhere to be *free* and *freaky*. For an entire weekend, we owned the city by parking our cars on the freeway, jumping into strange cars for photo ops, and drinking strange drinks all in the name of crazy fun.

It was at the beginning of my senior year; however, that caused me to take pause as my college career would soon be over. Clark Atlanta University was a rich college experience in enjoying all that it had to offer, including occasional dating, but there was no steady boyfriend. In attending college, there was not only a degree in mind but a future husband as well. Since the latter had not yet come to pass, I concocted a plan in hopes that it would change my status. Clark Atlanta University was a part of the Atlanta University Center which comprised three other HBCUs including Morris Brown College, Spelman College where Esther Rolle attended in the 1940s, and Morehouse College, a historically, private, all-male black college.

Because we were a part of this educational system, colleges would allow students to 'cross register,' which meant students can register and enroll at other colleges in the Atlanta University Center (AUC). As an English major, I decided to take a course at Morehouse College.

Father always said, "Never chase a man. Let the man chase you."

Father was right but I didn't see anything wrong in putting myself in a man's way for him to catch me.

To help in my quest, I approached a college friend from Indiana to be my partner in crime. We decided on taking an English course at Morehouse from a male professor whose wife was one of our English professors at Clark Atlanta University. When we arrived at his class on the first day of school, some of the Morehouse students who had already registered began to take a seat.

When approaching the professor for written permission to be in his class, he breaks the bad news. "I can't accept any more students for this class. I have reached my capacity."

Just then, I turned my head and did a double take at a handsome, very tall, dark-skinned male wearing what appeared to be a lettered basketball jacket and thought, he could possibly be the husband that I prayed for. The professor's response was getting in my way. Thinking fast on my feet, I said to the professor, "We must take this class. We're seniors and need it to graduate. Can you please give us an override?"

An override was a form given by professors that accepted a student for special circumstances in spite of a class maximum capacity. He granted our request.

We always looked forward to walking over to Morehouse for our English class as well as seeing my crush who was a Morehouse basketball player. Being inspired, I even wrote a poem about him secretly and entitled it "The Ocean" using metaphorical language to express my feelings. I recited it in class and even got an 'A' on the assignment.

My crush was so impressed by it until he asked me to help him with one of the English assignments that he missed due to a basketball game. With butterflies in my stomach, I said "Sure!" in looking forward to our tutorial session. "I really appreciate you helping me with this," he said.

"I would love for us to talk more. Are you available for lunch next Monday, around 1:00 p.m.?"

Of course, my calendar was free even if it wasn't.

He then said that he would give me a call around 12:30 p.m. to confirm our date. My Morehouse plans of finding a mate were starting to pay off and with great anticipation, I looked forward to our date.

Monday could not arrive soon enough. My calendar was clear as early as 10:30 a.m. so that I can be fixed in my dorm room to be available for my 12:30 p.m. call. Dressed to a 'tee', I couldn't wait to get my phone call from my soon-to-be boyfriend. When 12:30 p.m. arrived, there was no call but everybody needs a little grace time. 12:45 p.m. came and still no phone call. 1:00 p.m. came and went as I checked the phone line to see if my phone was plugged to the necessary connections. 1:30 p.m. arrived and I began to offer excuses for him that something could've happened which prevented him from calling. When 2:00 p.m. rolled around, my temper flared as I began to grasp the hard truth that I had been "stood-up."

A call from my basketball crush was never received but I did receive one from Father who could instinctively tell that something was wrong.

"How are things going?" Father asked.

I curtly responded, "Fine!"

Father began to inquire more as I told him the truth about being stood-up. "You can't let him get away with that," he exclaimed. "He was wrong! You've got to confront that negro about it!"

Though hurt, I never thought about confronting my crush in his wrongdoing and any kind of stand-off of that sort was out of my comfort zone.

"You're not confronting him in trying to get him back. You're confronting him so he doesn't do another woman like he did you! Just listen to me, you're going to see him on campus and when you do, tell him how you feel! "

Father was right. Soon after, I spotted him talking with a young lady.

His eyes grew large as he saw me approach him.

Abruptly, I interrupted his conversation, "We need to talk!" I then told him how I felt in a firm but non-explicit way. He listened, and offered no explanation. When finished, I walked away 'free' inside, knowing that I did the right thing. About a week later, my used-to-be crush found me and offered apologies which I accepted.

When Father heard the news, his response was that of gratefulness, "Good. You did it... You've forgiven him and now you can move on. Besides, there's more fish in the sea!"

Father was wrong on that part. It didn't feel like more "fish in the sea" and with my soon-to-be departure from my African American collegiate waters, the possibility of catching a *good black sea bass* would appear to be less and less. My husband dream was deferred; however, I was able to complete my studies in the four years as planned, graduating with a Bachelor of Arts (B.A.) in English with a once again honor status.

My LIVING SINGLE

After graduation, it was time for me to move out of the dorm. In one sense, life was good because I had a college degree. In another sense, I was lost in that I had no concrete direction in what to do with it or even myself.

My mother inquired of my plans, "So what are you going to do now? Are you planning to come back home to Orlando? Your father is making plans to come and pick you up and bring you back here!"

Certainly, I didn't want to go back home to Orlando. In love with Atlanta, I wanted to make it my home for good. Besides, I thought, if I went back home, my chances of living in Atlanta again were slim to none. This is when I discovered that life will present choices in which one is required to make a major decision and it is the road that you choose which can determine your destiny. Somehow, I had to take a leap of faith and stay in Atlanta, but where?

My mother offered her advice, "Call your aunt and see if she would let you stay there."

My aunt was Mother's younger sister who looked almost identical to her but was a foot shorter in stature. She along with her husband, my uncle, lived in Southwest Atlanta a.k.a. SWAT off of Sylvan Road which was a main street in the area. My aunt wore a short carefree curl and worked in housing as a mortgage counselor who helped persons remain in their homes during economic hardships. She was also an evangelist in the Church of God in Christ (COGIC) while my uncle, who often wore a light blue cap tilted to the side of his head, was a no-nonsense retired mechanic. Though confined to a wheelchair as a diabetic amputee, he was always timely in taking his insulin, kept a loaded gun in his right pocket, and didn't have a "lazy bone" in his body, often cooking for the family.

According to their backgrounds, they were an unlikely pair but they were clearly in love as exemplified with their flirtatious humor and wit. All in all, they were good people for as they opened their doors to the neighborhood in selling candy, which supported my aunt's church, they also opened their doors in allowing me to stay with them.

Church was not a priority for me during my collegiate years. Though I sporadically visited a few churches, I never made a commitment to any of them. Being out of Mother's home, I was not forced to go to church. It felt good being able to hide my 'PK' status and remain unidentified unless spoken by me. This was a privilege that was never experienced before in Orlando. Back home, every black person who went to anybody's church knew Mother or Father. While in college, whenever my parents would make mention of it, I always knew how to say the appropriate words for an excuse. Now, being a college graduate, Father would confront me about my spirituality, "I know you're not going to church, young lady, but' you need to go now. You need God and church to make it in this world. There's a good friend of mine who pastors a good church. You should go this Sunday."

The church was the oldest African American church in Atlanta being founded in 1847 by slaves and sat in the heart of Auburn Avenue. It had been called the "Jesus Saves" Church because it was the only church in Atlanta that shone the words in neon atop the prominent cross and steeple. One could see it from the I-75/85 expressway that passed through the city. On the following Sunday, I drove to the church in my 1983 brown Buick Regal, which was one of Father's cars that he gave me upon college graduation. Father had always bought Lincoln Town Cars but upon seeing this low-mileage/low-cost, used Buick Regal, he couldn't pass up a good deal, using it as his side car. Immediately, I drove it with pride, noticing that my car was in a class by itself as Cadillacs, Mercedes Benzes, BMWs, and other like models made their way to the church parking lot. Fine cars never intimidated me.

My Buick and I held our own as I exited the car and made my way inside the church. Being greeted with warm personalities, I was smitten by the architectural design of the sanctuary which comprised a rotunda style structure adorned with stained glass windows, and all of the trimmings. It was the most beautiful church I had ever seen. The atmosphere was spiritually high and the preached word was soul stirring. After worship, I introduced myself to the pastor and first lady who were both very hospitable in their gestures and in their familiarity with Father. The pastor inquired more in asking about my plans after college in which I stated that I wanted to use my English degree to go into broadcast journalism.

A few Sundays later, after joining the church, the Pastor said something that would change my life. He asked one of the members who was an executive vice president for Turner Broadcasting System to talk with me about a job. I could feel it. It was a Kairos—God moment where I would serve as a beneficiary.

The woman was very kind as she jotted down my information only to call me the next day to inform me of a position within the professional basketball organization at the CNN building. She said, "The job title is Community Affairs Trainee. It pays only $5.50/hour but it comes with major benefits. It will also put your foot in the door to pursue your journalism career. Now, understand it's highly competitive but you should have no problem. Do well on the interview, they are waiting for you." Certainly, I was in the real world now, becoming a witness to the true statement, 'Networking is not only about who you know but also who knows you.' The interview went well—really well, as I felt like the job was mine even before they offered it.

Along with a new job, there came a new name, sort of. Earlier in life, I was primarily called by my middle name 'Clara' instead of my first name 'Annie.' Being named after Mother, family and friends would call me 'Clara' and refer to Mother as 'Ann' for a differentiator. In my book, 'Ann' was more classy and stylish than 'Clara.' Now as an adult with a professional job, I officially decided to take matters into my hands and become the 'Ann Champion' that I always dreamed of.

Though I carried a stature of a woman who plays basketball, standing at 5'10", I was never interested in playing the game. However, I was a huge fan of it. During that time, I was in emotional basketball recovery from the devastating hometown loss, where in the 1995 Finals, my Orlando team would fall short of winning the championship. Now, I was cheering for a different team and working at a cool job that I would've never imagined in a million years.

As with other parts of Atlanta, the feeling of black presence and pride was throughout this basketball organization as well. This overflowed into the leadership of the Community Affairs Dept. where my director would be a 1968 Olympics Track Gold Medalist. Some of the job details included helping to organize the ball signing events for charity organizations, A Golf and Tennis Classic, along with other clerical duties. There was the privilege of receiving courtside season tickets to witness the play action of basketball greats such as Charles Barkley and Michael Jordan. Also, there was the sweet opportunity to usher at the 1995 World Series. It was a treat to see David Justice hit the single homeroom to win Atlanta the baseball crown.

One of the friendliest celebrities that I met while working there was Whitman Mayo. Whitman drove a purple Porsche and starred on the hit TV show, *Sandford and Son*. After the internship ended, my appetite changed from journalism to theater. I had caught 'the acting bug' and pursued this endeavor by joining a small acting company. Informing Whitman of my acting interests, he was very kind in offering advice and even attended a production where I had a leading role. He encouraged me to continue my studies at graduate school for my Masters in Fine Arts if this was something that I really wanted to pursue. Following suit, I applied to UCLA's Master of Fine Arts (MFA) Program where it was required to go to New York for an audition.

Informing Father of my theatrical interests, he served as my number one cheerleader.

"I'm so glad that you're doing this!" he said. "Who knows, maybe you can be the next Cicely Tyson or Esther Rolle?"

Whenever you're trying something new, stepping out into the deep, it helps to have motivation and encouragement especially from family. Giving it the old college try, I auditioned and felt confident about my performance. Returning home, I awaited their response where disappointment would come in receiving a "we regret to inform you" letter. More so, my one-year trainee/internship program would come to an end with no job offers in sight. Placed on pause, my professional future anywhere was uncertain.

They say at eighteen, you're legally an adult but not truly 'grown' until you have your own place and pay your own bills.

After living with my aunt and uncle for sixteen months, she said, "It's time to get your own place."

Unhappy with her statement, I leaned on George and his wife to take me in.

George and my sister-in-law had recently relocated to Atlanta from Orlando. George, who had taken on other jobs prior including concert promotor and car salesman, was now working as another kind of salesman in health fitness. George seemed to be a natural fit for sales even convincing me to purchase a fitness contract that I later regretted. For the brief time I was there, he and my sister-in-law were kind and considerate especially when my 1983 Buick Regal was stolen from their driveway. As the police drove up to the crime scene, George was there with a hug and words of consolation.

"I'm sorry sis. They'll get your car back," George said.

"I hope so," I sadly responded.

When someone steals your car, it's a feeling of violation, invasion. These were feelings that I had experienced before under different circumstances. My Buick was soon recovered though no longer the same. After six months of residing with George and my sister-in-law, I finally elevated to the 'grown woman' status by moving into my own place.

Later, I thanked my aunt Dorothy for telling me it was time to move out. She and my uncle offered their home as a temporary not permanent measure to help me get on my feet. Her tough love propelled me to get my act together and become the strong black *independent* woman that I needed to be.

Unlike the *Living Single* television sitcom, where four women shared a Brooklyn Brownstone, my 'Living Single' would be a single unit apartment in Stone Mountain, GA. It sat in a remote, wooded area and its interior was accented with a stone-covered fireplace and sunroom making it a perfect place for an introvert like myself.

Family was concerned because of my decision to live alone.

My uncle believed in carrying a concealed weapon. He said, "You're a woman living in this world by yourself. You got to protect yourself. You need to get a gun." His point of reference was informed by the streets.

Father said the contrary. "You don't need a gun. You've got God and that's who will protect you." His point of reference was informed by his faith. Weighing both options, I chose the latter as I trusted God to protect me, and he did.

At the "Jesus Saves" Church, my spirituality grew deeper as I attended Bible Study more often and sang in the Purple Robe Choir. To quench my theatrical thirst, I became the narrator of their popular theater production, one of the longest running continuous plays in the nation. Even with my intricate involvement in the church, however, a vibrant social life was still maintained.

There was a popular event concert center located on Memorial Drive near Stone Mountain. Popular music artists would frequent and on this particular Saturday night, Erykah Badu, the R&B music sensation was the headliner. Badu was climbing the music charts with her hits "On and On" and "Tyrone," a song that most single women could identify in having dated a brother who had "Tyrone-like characters" hanging around him.

The place was filled to capacity. My girlfriends and I would not be disappointed in hearing Erykah's sounds and taking in all the male sights. There was one in particular that drew my interest. His hair wasn't the only thing that locked; so did our eyes as we both smiled in approval and stared long in realizing that we were already acquainted. Earlier in college, he and I dated momentarily, not even remembering why we parted, but due to his new and improved physicality, it really didn't matter. We then exchanged hugs and conversation as we delved into a dating world which also included his popular megachurch that was located in Lithonia, GA. "I'm not as wild as I used to be," he said. "I've changed." I could tell. Time changes all of us in some shape, form or fashion.

Some changes are for the good and some are for the not so good. We both made good changes in our relationship with God. It was a wonderful experience, visiting his popular church with his popular pastor who was a nationally known bishop. When visiting, we made sure that we arrived an hour early so our chances of getting a parking space were good. Eagerness and excitement filled the atmosphere as worshippers entered his megachurch. Admittedly, it was something special that one could see as read on the faces of the people. Truly, they were going to receive some kind of special blessing.

One Sunday, his bishop extended the invitation for persons to join the church. My friend remarked. "Come on and join," he said with a cunning smile. "I'll walk down there with you." His proposition made for good motivation but not sound judgment. After all, I now had a special connection with the "Jesus Saves" Church not just due to Father's reference but because I personally had developed relationships, worked in various ministries and had now claimed it as truly my own.

After three months or more of dating, our schedules didn't align. His occupation kept him busy in his world and my occupation kept me busy in mine. We also discovered that we were equally saved but not equally yoked as our backgrounds, values, principles began to unfold differently. Sooner than later, our joy ride was over. It was time to get off and move on for good.

* * *

Something strange was happening to me in the fall of 1997. By now, I was working as a news technician for a construction information new company as I had found this job in the classified section of the *Atlanta Journal and Constitution* newspaper. My English degree was now paying off as my salary was almost $30K, which was a long way from the $5.50/hr. trainee position. Being somewhat comfortable in this position, I didn't mind the heavy traffic in traveling east from Stone Mountain to Ashford-Dunwoody Rd. to get there. However, I was earnestly inquiring of God for purpose and direction in life especially after that failed theatrical attempt with UCLA. It felt like there was something BIG that God wanted me to do but I couldn't place exactly what it was. "Be careful of what you ask for," someone once said, "you just might get it."

God showed me. One day, as I was praying, a voice informed me to get the Bible and open it up. I opened it and my eyes landed on Joel 2:28 "And it shall come to pass, I will pour out my spirit on all people. Your sons and daughters will prophesy…" With shock and fright, I immediately closed the Bible as I shook my head feverishly in disapproval of the revelation or what others refer to as "The Call."

"Oh no, God! Oh no!" I said. "I can't do that. Please don't ask me to do that… Please don't ask me to preach."

I then bargained. "I'll be a first lady. I can do that but I can't preach!"

God ignored my request. "Preach my Word!" kept resonating within me.

From then on, there was an internal wrestle in my spirit and I was on the run trying to ignore the ONE that called Father and generations before him. The voice, "Preach my Word" even followed me to my job as it proved to be overwhelming and inescapable. At this point, I had to entrust someone with my information so I nervously called Father with the news.

"Daddy I've got something to tell you." I could hear him holding his breath as he was waiting for me to continue. "I think I've been called to preach."

There was a heavy sigh of relief and then a comical comment from Father, "Thank God! I thought you were about to tell me you were pregnant!"

I blurted, "Daddy no… I'm pregnant but not with a baby!" We laughed only briefly as our conversation took on a more serious tone.

"Daughter… you've been called…"

"Yes," I responded softly.

"That's a marvelous thing! A glorious thing!" It was how he said it.

Father had this dramatic flair and demeanor that I inherited honestly. We continued to talk as I gently wept in sharing my spiritual episodes. Father agreed to keep it a secret as he offered prayer and said that he would call me the next morning. It was the most peaceful, sound sleep that I had in a long time.

The next morning, I was awakened by a phone call but it was not the voice of Father; instead, it was the voice of my elder cousin, whom we called "Big D." His nickname represented his last name and large physical stature as he not only pastored a megachurch in Savannah, GA but was the son of my great-aunt, Rev. Chestina Williams Delaney, who began her ministry in the 1950s when only a handful of women were ordained. He considered himself our family's lead minister in representing the more than 50 preachers in our bloodline.

"Congratulations!" he said proudly and loudly. "You answered the call!"

In other words, he was saying, "Welcome to the family business."

Father could never keep a secret and I should've known that. After he finished expressing his elation, Father soon called.

"I thought we were going to keep it a secret for now," I told Daddy.

"How do you feel after our conversation from last night?" he asked, deflecting from my comment.

"I feel good. I actually feel *FREE*," I said.

"That's because it's out of you… you've spoken it… you've released it! I'm so happy I don't know what to do!" Father responded.

After talking with Father, I called Mother to share the good news. Afterwards, I informed my pastor who provided spiritual counseling for my new journey. My initial sermon was held in May of next year where family and close friends attended, including George who offered his congratulations and good job commendations. There were others who gave their initial sermons as well.

The female ministers formed a bond where we had our own ministerial sorority, cynically calling ourselves 'The Bethel Angels.' The name was tailored after the TV sitcom *Charlie's Angels*, where instead of carrying guns for weapons, we had our bibles and each other's backs. As single 'preach-hers' aged in our 20s and 30s, our dress style was contemporary and at times, criticized by older females, who felt our suit skirts were just a little too high above the knees. When approached, we stood our ground, determined to be our authentic selves, even if it agitated the status quo. The most refreshing fact was that women all over the world were bold in standing uniquely for God in answering their ministerial call. Entering seminaries by the droves, I would join some of these "called" women at Emory University, Candler School of Theology in the fall of 1998.

My Emory education would find its way through the corridors of Bishop's Hall, which was the main administrative building for Candler School of Theology. Though Candler was a predominately white seminary, it sought inclusion and diversity, and it was refreshing to see a solid number of African Americans who attended. Even on the faculty, African Americans professors brilliantly led and taught various theological and homiletical subject matter. At one point, Nobel Peace Prize Winner, Archbishop Desmond TuTu even served as a visiting professor in a class entitled "God and Us: Introduction to Contextual Theology and Ministry." It was an honor to be in his class to study and learn about South Africa's journey toward freedom and justice. While matriculating at Candler, there were even opportunities for me to travel with the World Methodist Evangelism Institute where I not only got the chance to minister in other parts of the world but to also visit places like 'Stonehenge' in Wiltshire, England.

Initially, seminary was overwhelming as I tried to make sense of this new reality as well as the call to preach. My spirit was in an endless wrestle for a few reasons. First, while witnessing two prior preacher generations undergo church burdens and bad board meetings, it made me hesitant to follow in their footsteps. Secondly, my status was single, falling short of any man "putting a ring on it" anytime soon. Lastly, there were feelings of not being worthy for this job called 'PREACHER.'

It wasn't until attending board of examiners, which consists of an ordained ministerial panel within my denomination, that I would get clarity. One of my instructors was an experienced woman in ministry who was not only a mother of twin sons and a gifted pastor, but a wise counselor as well. She had each student to stand and give their call story. As I presented mine, she offered words of encouragement, "You are enough," she said. "God knows who you are now and knew who you were when he called you. I also hear your acknowledgment of the call to others but I have not heard your acceptance of the call to God... Have you told God YES?" Silent and teary-eyed, I was emotional because she was right. Clearly, I was going through the motions of ministry but had not actually told God 'YES' because of my issues. Shaking my head as if to say 'no', the instructor offered the opportunity for me to get things right. Bowing my head, I prayed my acceptance call to the ONE that mattered the most.

The Interdenominational Theological Center (ITC) is a consortium of five predominately African American denominational seminaries that is a part of the Atlanta University Center (AUC). In the 1960s, Father was a student there and went on to serve as the Dean of Turner Theological Seminary which were primary reasons why he wanted me to attend this seminary instead of Emory, Candler. Though initially disgruntled by my seminary decision, he eventually had a change of heart and was even happier to know that I had taken a couple of ITC courses.

My last semester before graduating from Emory Candler, I decided to enroll in another course at ITC. This time, I would take a preaching course. The professor would always teach the importance of creativity in sermon writing by using terms as 'painting the picture' so our audience could actually visualize our message. His class would prove to be different by no stretch of the imagination. As each student preached, the professor allowed for musical accompaniment which is a style called "bump," a term that describes short clips of music that is intermittently played to promote spirituality in the preaching moment. Amazed and dlighted, I enjoyed the vivacious, spiritual responses from the other students, making it a different seminarian experience from what I was used to at Emory Candler.

After preaching my sermon in class, there was a student who offered commendation and told me that he was organizing a special worship service at his church.

"I'm having a preacher-thon service at my church which will consists of (7) preachers....Will you be one of them?" he asked.

After checking my schedule, I gave my confirmation.

"Who are the other preachers?" I asked.

He offered male names whom I did not know but then he said one that sounded familiar, "Robert Shaw."

As he said his name, I thought to myself, *what a surprise… Robert Shaw, I've heard of him.*

THE GOOD TIMES

Good Times Actress Esther Rolle in Sunday Worship at St. Mark, Orlando, FL December, 1979. Left to Right: My father and senior pastor, Rev. Dr. George Lovelace Champion, Sr., Esther Rolle, Rev. Lugenia Sanchez, and Rev. James D. Gordon, Jr.

Sunday Afternoon Dinner at the St. Mark parsonage with Esther Rolle. Left to Right: Rev. Lugenia Sanchez, Esther Rolle, my father, Rev. Dr. George Lovelace Champion, Sr., and my mother, Mrs. Annie Clara White Champion.

THE GOOD TIMES

As First Lady of St. Mark, Mother loved Christmas and fashion. Here, she is wearing one of her outfits with a leopard hat.

Paternal grandparents: Rev. George Maurice Champion, pastor and church builder of St. Paul AME Church, Ft. Pierce, FL and Mrs. Annie Mae Williams Champion would often visit us at the St. Mark parsonage.

Mother gave the best birthday parties. My 6th Birthday with St. Mark friends. Left to Right: Katrina Edwards and Kimberly J. Sweeting.

THE GOOD TIMES

Riding in Father's Lincoln was always an experience. Here, Father dons his signature beret hat while my big sister, Tymy M. Champion looks on.

One of our family trips included a visit to Washington, DC. Mother and I outside of the White House, July 1981.

Our FAMILY MATTERS

My big brother, Rev. George L. Champion, Jr. finished his high school years at John I. Leonard High School, Lake Worth, FL. Here, he is running track as a senior in Spring, 1986.

WHAT'S HAPPENING to us?

Senior year at Jones High School, Orlando, Florida. The Coronation. Miss Concert Choir, 1990-1991.

My best friends of Jones High School were confidants and comic relief. This is us in 1990 on canvas. Sitting left to right: Terri Rucker Hargrove, Shirley Foster Brown. Standing left to right: Myself, Tessine J. Moses

It's a DIFFERENT WORLD

When moving to Atlanta, my aunt, Dorothy White Gamble was loving and supportive in my transition. Here is myself, Aunt Dorothy, and Mother in December 1992.

Attending HBCU Clark Atlanta University was one of the best decisions I ever made. College graduation, May 1995. Left to Right: Myself, Rev. Micki Reid-Benson, and Stacye Bishop Langford.

My LIVING SINGLE

Me at Stonehenge, Wiltshire, England, January 2001.

Smiles with Archbishop Desmond TuTu, Emory Candler School of Theology, Spring 2000.

Graduation Day. Emory Candler School of Theology, May 2001. Smiles with my Delta aunts. Left to Right: Jessie Champion Jenkins and Patience Champion Mitchell.

My LIVING SINGLE

We began our ministry together at Big Bethel AME "Jesus Saves" Church, Atlanta GA. In May 2001, we were ordained as itinerant deacons in the African Methodist Episcopal (AME) Church. Left to Right: Rev. Dr. Michelle Rizer-Poole, Myself, CH (COL) Monica R. Lawson, and Rev. Maria Mallory White

Father was my cheerleader in life and ministry. My ordination as an itinerant elder in the AME Church, May 2003.

Our For BETTER or For WORSE

I met "Mr. Right" Robert Shaw at a preacher-thon in Atlanta, GA on April 8, 2001. Seminarians from The Interdenominational Theological Center (ITC) who were there. Left to Right: Myself, Rev. Dr. Will D. Hayes, III, Rev. Robert Ryland Shaw, II, Rev. James Turner, II, and Rev. Dr. Jason L. Robinson.

Robert and his best man, best friend, brother, Bryan A. Shaw, Sr. stay cool before the wedding.

Wedding smiles after the ceremony with my college roommate, best friend and maid of honor Angelitos (Angie) L. Lipscomb at Big Bethel AME "Jesus Saves" Church, Atlanta, GA.

Our For BETTER
or For WORSE

Rob and I sharing a tender moment before our wedding reception on July 19, 2003.

Our wedding reception was held at my alma mater, Clark Atlanta University, which served as my point of entry into Atlanta twelve years earlier.

MEET THE SHAWS

My best friends Tessine J. Moses and Shirley Foster Brown from Orlando, Florida surprised me for my 30th Birthday in Kansas City, MO. It was the best one yet.

Me and Mother-in-love, Willa A. Spears Shaw in Albuquerque, New Mexico for a Women's Prayer Conference, May 2004.

STRONG ROOTS

Maternal grandparents: Charlie George (CG) White, Sr. and Tymy M. Hartage White of Ellaville, GA at their 60th Wedding Anniversary, December 1992. My grandmother was a 'PK' who was born and raised in the AME Church.

Maternal great-grandparents: Rev. George Washington Hartage and Mrs. Laura Battle Hartage were the co-founders of Samuel "Sammy" Chapel AME Church, Buena Vista (Marion County), GA. Picture taken around 1950.

Digesting SOUL FOOD

Father hanging out with his grandchildren, Robert Ryland Shaw, III (1 month old) and Raven Noel Lovelace Shaw, (3 years old) at the Allen Chapel parsonage, Kansas City, MO, March 2008.

Hey THAT'S MY MAMA

Mother was filled with joy in seeing her granddaughter Raven for the first time. Allen Chapel parsonage, Kansas City, MO, Feb. 2005.

Me looking at my Queen Mother as she enjoys herself at the Joy and Jazz event in St. Louis, MO, October 2010.

Here I am offering words of remembrance at Mother's funeral in St. Mark, Orlando, FL, April 18, 2015.

Let the Church Say AMEN

Tymy on the stairwell of her home in Kansas City, MO.

George and son, Dyrell J. Brown in 2016.

Let the Church Say AMEN

Rob preaching his first Sunday as Senior Pastor of Bethel AME Church, San Francisco on a ladder, Oct. 8, 2017.

First Day of Catholic school in San Francisco. Raven—7th Grade and Robert III (Robby)—4th Grade, January 2018.

Me and My Heartbeats. The Shaws in San Francisco 2018.

Our For BETTER or For WORSE

I first heard of him through my sister in ministry at the "Jesus Saves" Church.

A month or so earlier, she said, "Robert Shaw told me to tell you hello."

"I don't know him," I responded. Her comment left me puzzled yet piqued my curiosity in expressing my unfamiliarity with the individual.

She proceeded. "He's my classmate at ITC. He said you wouldn't know him. He just wanted to tell you hello."

The sentiment left me with a pause and the name of a man who will now get to tell me 'Hello' for himself.

The church where this Preacher-Thon would take place was on the southeast side of Atlanta, GA. The service was set to begin at 4:00 p.m. but I would arrive at 3:50 p.m. which was not unusual for a johnny-come-lately like myself. As I walked in the church, I was directed to the preachers' pew that was in the back as one by one each unfamiliar preacher stood up to greet me until at last I met *him*.

"Robert Shaw," he said with a rich baritone voice.

"Ann Champion… It's good to put a name with a face."

We smiled but only briefly as our host classmate quickly informed us that the worship service was due to begin.

"Ladies first," Robert said.

Leading the preachers down the aisle to the front row of reserved seats, Robert sat right beside me, of course.

It was the most *interesting* worship service in that there appeared to be orchestrated praise dance interludes between each sermon which included sounds from an extremely loud Hammond organ and whistle blowers. During it all, Robert and I would often give each other strange stares in experiencing our surroundings. Three hours into worship service and with three more sermons to be preached, I was most grateful in choosing cornrow braids as my hairstyle of choice while sweat ran down my brow with us becoming increasingly overwhelmed with the spiritual level that had risen to maximum capacity. In avoiding heat exhaustion, water was necessary so an exit strategy was put in place, but only temporary as I had not yet preached.

After walking out to the vestibule, Robert followed suit. As we both got a drink and cooled down, I finally got a chance to look at my borderline stalker who had observed me from afar in sending messages through my friend. In noticing his features, close up and personal, mental notes were taken of his smooth chocolate skin and sweet smile, but there was one issue, he looked young, younger than myself.

"How old are you sweetheart?" I asked condescendingly.

"How old do you think I am?" he responded with a smirk after a pause, as if he had to hold back his words from saying something he might regret.

I responded, "Twenty-two or twenty-three."

He laughed and then said, "Twenty-seven."

"Wow…we're the same age!?" I said.

We both were surprised as I thought he was younger and he assumed I was of a more mature age.

"You thought I was older. Didn't you?" I inquired.

He would deny it, however, a smart man with a baby face.

Returning to the sanctuary, I finally preached my sermon as the Preacher-thon would end over seven hours later from its scheduled start. This set my personal book of world records for the longest worship service that I had ever attended. After worship, Robert and I engaged in banter and laughs from our long *whimsical* night. As he walked me to my car, he asked if he could call me as I responded with various excuses. Mother once told me that there are many ways to tell a man 'no.' This was one of them as he soon got the point and walked away.

It had been a year since I had dated as I was enjoying my sacred time with God. Now more focused on my ministry than ever before, my fear was that someone in my life at this season, would take me off course. More so, it was the first time where I truly felt a sense of wholeness without the accompaniment of a man. Feeling good, I didn't want to mess that up, especially with a smooth-talking preacher.

He stayed on my mind though. Even days after our encounter, I would think of Robert and wonder his status. Father always said "Let a man call you first." In living by this creed, I needed help to get him the message that in spite of what was initially said, I was interested. We both had good friends who were dating each other at the time and knew our situation, so they served as our mediator. It worked, as Robert soon called.

Our first phone conversation felt like forever as we talked into the wee hours of the night as though we had known each other all of our lives. Our phone calls soon resulted in dates to the museum, drive-in movies, and even roller blading where he was much more experienced than I was. We shared dinners at fine restaurants and soul food joints as I was taken with his HBCU experience at Prairie View A&M University, Prairie View, TX. His experiences as a Residential Director of Hubert Hall, Morehouse College was amusing and we both enjoyed analyzing and listening to sermons and music. R&B music artist Jill Scott's hit song, "A Long Walk," described us perfectly.

I'd heard him preach at the Preach-her-thon but he shared the pulpit with other preachers including me. One Sunday morning, he would have the preaching moment all to himself. Robert was on the ministerial staff at a church whom I called 'The Cathedral' that was located in East Atlanta, a suburb called Decatur. Years earlier, I had visited this church. Its membership had a friendly and warm demeanor that mirrored its pastor who served the congregation for over 30 years. growing it from 200 members to well over 10,000.

When I arrived at the church, I encountered George, who was now single. George was an active member of the congregation as he was led there by Father, who was good friends with the pastor. It was like a fraternal bond where pastors would automatically know to look out for other PKs who were a part of their membership. This happened for George at 'The Cathedral' like it happened for me at the "Jesus Saves" Church. Like myself,

George was now called into ordained ministry as he had given his initial sermon a year after I did.

As I sat next to George during the service, he inquired of my presence. "Why are you here today, Sis?"

"I just wanted to worship with my big brother," I replied. He didn't believe me, of course, but he didn't object. George would soon figure me out and discover my real motive for being there.

While looking in the pulpit, I noticed Robert sitting in the "Big Chair." This is the name given as the chair for the minister who will preach the sermon for that particular worship service. Robert gave me a wink and nodded to confirm he noticed my presence. Service went on as normal and when it was time for the preaching moment, Robert had a great introduction.

"An orator is defined as a sophisticated rhetorician who is inebriated with the exuberance of his own verbosity… That's not me. I'm just one who is called by the Father, saved by the Son, and sent by the Holy Spirit."

His sermon was off to a great start and there was more as he received plenty of 'Amens,' 'Glories,' and 'Hallelujahs' from others as well as myself.

When I jumped up on one of my adulations, George received his revelation. "Oh! I know why you're here!" he said as he laughed to himself. George knew me like most siblings know each other. There is a personality truth in who we really are and what we really like that is known to the other. The truth will never be hidden for long. George figured me out so I told him about my new beau.

One of the members at the "Jesus Saves" Church once said, "A woman needs to spend at least four seasons with a man before she thinks about marrying him." For her, it was imperative that a woman spent an adequate amount of time with a man by knowing his true character before deciding to spend the rest of her life with him. For me, Rob had passed the seasons test. He and I had even survived an argument where we used words that would never be said in a pulpit. We always made up quickly as we were in love. In the fall of 2002, Rob would prove it when he proposed to me on bended knee with friends and family, including George, who served as a witness.

Life was changing really fast both personally and professionally with Robert being assigned as a senior pastor to a church in his hometown of Kansas City, Missouri. By societal norms, we were now engaged. By legal standards, our status was still single. This could prove to be problematic, especially with a single black male pastor serving a congregation.

Father had a solution to our problem as he always did in offering unsolicited advice. "This Sunday, let Robert go to his new church by himself. Now, on next Sunday, you need to show up so all the ladies who might be interested can close their pocketbooks."

"Daddy!" I said in response to his indecorous comment of 'close their pocketbooks.'

"I'm just trying to help you, daughter!" he said in his own defense.

The next Sunday I attended the worship service with Robert, who introduced me as the future Rev. Mrs. Shaw. The congregation was welcoming and the younger women seemed rather congenial. In observation, I did not sense any animosity, or maybe I was too oblivious in noticing any who were possibly interested in Robert. It didn't matter. Robert and I were happy and we couldn't wait to make it official.

Someone once said, "You don't marry the person you can live with—you marry the person you can't live without." I couldn't live without Robert and this feeling caused anxiety during our long-distance engagement as we hastily prepared for a wedding that was to take place in eight months. With so many details that go in planning a wedding, if possible, it is always wise to seek help. In soliciting assistance from one of the "Jesus Saves" Church members, she served as my wedding coordinator. She was very helpful in offering advice, especially in finding the best wedding deals on flowers.

The next big decision was choosing the bridal party. Robert would choose eight groomsmen which included his college roommates from Prairie View A & M University, Prairie View, TX, as well as his seminary preacher friends who called themselves 'The Elements': Earth, Wind, Fire, and Water, where each was nicknamed the element closest to their personality type. George would be one of the groomsmen as well. My eight bridesmaids would include Tymy as well as other family and girlfriends who were 'true' friends in every stage of my life. They all were beautiful, cool, funny, trustworthy, and understanding, especially when it came to their botched bridesmaids dresses which bared a strong resemblance to that of a house robe created by a faux fashion designer. Most of all, they were patient as we worked feverishly in finding a bridesmaid dress that was wedding worthy.

Before this fiasco, Mother gave space, allowing me the freedom to plan the wedding with the coordinator. After getting a sneak peak of Tymy's bridesmaid dress debacle, she hurriedly volunteered to make things better.

Mother called in distress. "Baby, how can I help? Please let me know!"

"No worries, Mama! Things will be handled," I assured her.

Father was sought for consolation and words of encouragement. "Don't worry about your wedding. It will be beautiful regardless of the attire. You have two lives coming together as one. That's beautiful but it's just one day. Pray for your marriage which you want to last a lifetime."

My prayers would go for the wedding first with the marriage in a distant second, as I needed eight bridesmaid dresses diverse in sizes 4 to 24 quick, fast, and in a hurry to meet our wedding date which was scheduled in a month. God answers prayers as a wedding shop located in northeast Atlanta had just what we needed to save our Big Day.

On my Big Day, not only did I need a wedding coordinator and bridal party, but I also needed a personal assistant/time manager. This position would keep my nerves calm and make sure that I would arrive to my wedding *on time*. One of my best friends from Orlando was chosen as she was perfect for this position. She knew me well including my issue with *chronological time*. It's strange in that my business is prompt but my body has a hesitancy where it shows up a little later than scheduled. A behavior carried over from childhood.

"Hey Sis! You might be late for your funeral but you're going to be on time for this wedding!" she exclaimed.

"Yes ma'am!" I said with laughter in knowing that she would have me right where I needed to be and on time.

Just like clockwork, she knocked on my hotel suite door, actually a little earlier than expected but then again, punctual people always seem to function ahead of time. She helped to gather my wedding dress and other essentials that a bride would need on her wedding day. We would ride in the limousine then transition to my dressing room at "Jesus Saves" Church which was the site of the wedding. Before going outside, she offered the forecast, "The weatherman said it's going to be hot today— real hot so stay cool Bride to Be!" She was right for July 19th felt like the hottest day of the year as most summer days do in Atlanta. They didn't call it 'HOTlanta' for nothing. However, the heat that we felt on the outside would not compare to the heat that we were going to experience on the inside. We just didn't know it yet.

The air conditioner was out of order at "Jesus Saves" Church. A course from the TV series Tyler Perry's *For Better or Worse* that followed three couples highs and lows of dating and married life couldn't prepare us for this moment. Yes, Jesus saves us from our sins but nothing could save us from the heat as there were no electricians available to fix the situation. There is an old saying that goes "Happy is the bride whom the sun shines on." There was nothing happy about this blistery bride along with my sweltering wedding party who scattered in trying to find reprieve, while church officers placed fans in every part of the building which seemed to only circulate the heat even more. George was feeling the heat too and it showed in an outburst on the videographer who had the camera too close in George's space while trying to capture moments of the wedding day. "Man! It's too hot for all of that! Move on now!" he exclaimed as he wiped the sweat from underneath his newly grown ponytail.

To make matters worse, one of the guests found me and offered our first wedding gift, a book entitled *Single, Married, Separated and Life After Divorce* by Myles Monroe. The book came highly recommended because it helped her through a bad divorce. The heat must have fried her brain. Though it was a good book that helped her heal, a book with a title like that was not appropriate for any couple on their wedding day. Instead of a blessing, it felt like an ill omen. The vows *For Better or For Worse* were being put to the test even before the wedding ceremony began. "Stay cool—Bride to Be." The words from my best friend echoed in my head.

After makeup and dress, I sat down in the fellowship hall, which felt a little cooler than my dressing room, to have some personal time before the wedding began. Father would soon join me.

As we sat and talked, he asked, "What is the most important word in marriage?

"Love," I said immediately.

He said, "No."

"Happiness," I responded.

He shook his head as if saying no.

"Forgiveness," he said. "Forgiveness is the most important word in marriage. Robert is going to do some things that are going to hurt you." He then paused and continued, "and you are going to do some things that are going to hurt Robert but if you keep forgiving each other, then you both will be alright."

As he spoke to me, it was almost like he was speaking through me—prophetically as though he saw something that I couldn't quite see yet.

The wedding processional began with the wedding party making its way down the aisle. As Father and I walked, my eyes were focused on Robert. In my periphery, there were a swarm of white fans frantically waving back and forth hoping they would produce some kind of relief. While walking, I remained cool, possibly due to living in an air condition-less house in Orlando, which unbeknownst at the time, prepared me for this sizzling moment.

Robert appeared cool too while we met face to face with our bishops standing in front of us to offer our nuptials. As ordained ministers, we were glad to have them there. They both were wise men with a laid back, caring persona that made them well respected.

The bishop of my region gave directives in the flow of the wedding ceremony while the bishop of Robert's region offered the sermon with one of the best lines ever. "Learn how to turn 'Jesus Keep Me Near the Cross' off and turn Luther Vandross on!"

Robert and I smiled to each other in agreement.

The wedding guests responded loudly, "AMEN!"

This appeared momentarily to take our minds off the heat or made things even hotter depending on the perspective, especially when mentioning Luther Vandross music. The ceremony would come to an end as Robert and I, Mr. and Mrs., or Rev. and Revs., would lovingly recess down the aisle but not with all of our wedding party. During the ceremony, some of my bridesmaids had to sit down or be taken out due to heat exhaustion. To my surprise, however, Tymy was standing "like a champ" as if the heat didn't phase her one bit.

Clark Atlanta University would save us from this 'overheated spirit' that seemed to follow me from my impoverished days in Orlando to my BIG wedding day in Atlanta. CAU's student center would serve as the place of our wedding reception. The reception site was sentimental in that Clark Atlanta was the educational place where my Atlanta journey began, and now it will serve as the endearing place where my Atlanta story would end. When we walked into the ballroom, the decorations were beautifully set in place as the air condition greeted us with a strong hug that wrapped around our entire bodies. The bridesmaids recovered, the catered food was delicious, and the DJ had us grooving on the dance floor. Our wedding guests were now laughing and cha cha sliding as the heat was now a thing of the past while me and Robert's new life was of the present and future.

Our 'Big Day' would end but not without its lasting effects that seemed to stay on my mind even days after the wedding was over. Pouring every ounce of energy and emotion in the wedding, my recovery would take some time. Even after traveling from our honeymoon cruise, the details of the wedding still remained in my psyche.

While flying on the plane, Robert told me that I would talk in my sleep and say things in reference to the wedding. The passenger sitting next to us would look strangely at me in my "sleep talk" mode while Robert would come to my rescue. "She's fine sir... just going through wedding detox," Robert would jokingly say. My life was quickly transforming so I needed to come out of this wedding fog. As the plane landed on the tarmac, our address had now changed to a familiar city for Robert but a foreign place to me. Rock and Roll Singer Fats Domino was right. 'Kansas City Here I Come.'

MEET THE SHAWS

When we drove up to the home, I stopped and stared in knowing that I would be living in a parsonage just as I did in Orlando. . . The outside of both homes were similar in that both were red brick, but the difference was that the one in Orlando was ranch style while this was a three-story Kansas City home. Robert was determined to carry me over the threshold as we entered our new place of residence. We would enter our first home which consisted of hardwood floors with a beautiful gloss finish along with 3 bedrooms, living room, dining room, breakfast nook, closed-in patio, 2-door garage, and an office with a large bookcase that was big enough to contain the college, seminary, and other books that Robert and I had acquired over the years. Robert was especially excited about the basement in which he made plans to purchase a pool table for recreational time. Loving our new home, I couldn't wait to get to know his family—our family.

Robert's background was much different from mine. He was a second generation born and raised Kansas Citian having relatives on both sides of his family reside there. Robert attended Catholic schools and was raised in a two-parent home. His mother, Willa Shaw, was a tenured government employee while his father, Robert Shaw, who spoke with a distinctive voice similar to acclaimed actor James Earl Jones, was a retired baker from one of the local universities.

Robert only had one younger brother, Bryan. Both he and Bryan, an educator and then father of twins, shared a strong resemblance. Public opinion would often mistake one for the other. In the correction, the comment would always be "He's the Preacher and I'm the Teacher" or vice versa depending on who was saying it. Immediately, I became fond of their brotherly bond which was more like best friends, as whenever Bryan would stop by for a visit, he and Robert would steal away downstairs to the man cave for a game of pool.

Robert's family was large, very large, especially on his father's side where earlier generations had come from Douglas, Georgia. There was even a running joke about it where Robert would say, "If you meet someone black in Kansas City whose last name is Shaw, they are probably my cousin." I was beginning to meet lots and lots of them. With these gatherings would come smiles, good times, and laughter like a scene from Tyler Perry's *Meet the Browns*. Robert's blood family would extend to the communal where he had a hosts of 'aunts and uncles' that included close friends of the family.

The family's reference to each other in using nicknames was also endearing, especially when I learned that Robert was referred to as Robby. He wouldn't be the only family member that would share an 'e' sound at the end of their nickname. His late grandfather, whom they called Poppy, along with Uncle Nicky, Aunt Ebbie, Aunt Geri, Aunt Annie Bannie and more, shared this 'e' sound nickname ending as well. They were all good people being very helpful in my adjustment. The Shaws told me about the best restaurants including BBQ joints where one in particular would always greet their patrons with "How may I help you?" in a twang accent. Kimmie, one of Robert's cousins, even referred a great hair salon that weekly kept me up on my hair game.

Being married also meant being roommates as we were daily learning each other's lifestyle and personality. Robert had the classic husband bad habit of not putting the toilet lid down after use. Initially, this never bothered me as when I would see it up, I would put it down and then gently remind him of it. It wasn't until a half-sleep bathroom trip at 3:00 a.m. resulting in my bottom unwantedly sitting in a pool of toilet water that caused my outburst and Robert's apologies.

We also shared differing personalities, where he was an extrovert gaining stimulation by being around people, whereas I was an introvert in gaining stimulation with being by myself. Don't get me wrong, I loved hosting parties as it was a trait learned from Mother in St. Mark's parsonage, but knowing all the details including guests arrival and most importantly departure was essential for me. One day, our personality difference was put to test as we had prepared for a Shaw family gathering to watch the Chiefs, who in over three decades never seemed to make it past the second round of playoffs. Rob and I usually kept each other informed; however, there was miscommunication of more persons attending than expected, I panicked and we argued. Father told us earlier, "You won't always agree but don't let others see your drama. Keep it to yourselves." Our family and friends soon came over. We smiled and greeted them as though nothing happened. We talked and made up later.

We had a few differences, but we were newlyweds and our church would soon sense the passion that we had for each other. There was a time where our love met us on Saturday night and overflowed into a late Sunday morning, causing us to lose track of time. As Robert made a call to the head church officer explaining that "we overslept," we hurriedly drove to the church as I put my makeup on in the car. When entering the church, the vestibule was filled with folded arms and strange stares from our twenty-minute tardiness. Rob and I put on the cordiality with the "Good Mornings," "How is everybody," "Apologies for our tardiness." For some churches, like this one, there is a dependency upon pastors for everything so as far as worship leadership, it was us or nobody. After finally seeing us, our congregation slowly assembled in the sanctuary; however, the drag would be lifted as we had a high, celebratory service full of praise.

After worship, Rob and I thought we could leave an uncontested congregate confrontation regarding our temple tardiness, but a proper Sunday School teacher who wore her reading glasses on the tip of her nose would not let us get away with it. "Hey Reverends… I know how those Sunday mornings can be. I was young once, just schedule it a little better next time!" Embarrassed by her comment, we all laughed but we were never late again to church, at least for that reason.

My first winter in Kansas City was grueling as my body tried to acclimate to the wind chill factor. At this point, the coldest weather that I had ever been exposed to was in Atlanta where the coldest day was around 28 degrees. In Atlanta, if a meteorologist ever predicted snow and ice, it was an unofficial city holiday, and persons would make their way to the grocery store to refill their cupboards. While staying home, residents would catch up on sleep, reading, or other chores because all of the schools, businesses, and major roads would be closed due to insufficient snow plows. Not for Kansas City, they were equipped with the biggest and best snow plows, making no excuse for persons to drive to work or schools even in the worst climate conditions.

This southern girl was not used to this kind of weather not to mention driving in it. During the extremely frigid weather days, Rob would chauffeur me to my job at one of the nearby hospitals.

At the hospital, I worked as a chaplain in residence and was a part of the Clinical Pastoral Education (CPE) Program. Mother was happy in receiving the news, as she always preached, "Always keep a job, never depend on a man for anything." As a chaplain resident, we were required to be a part of the on-call rotation staying overnight at the hospital and keeping the pager on and near, just in case we had a midnight code blue or ER trauma. This work was cut out for adrenaline junkies as one would have to readily and proficiently respond to the unexpected, which could be grueling and intense—not for the faint of heart.

A few months after moving to Kansas City, I would celebrate my 30th birthday, being no longer in my twenties and yet having not reached full maturity. Somewhere, I was in the middle as was a strand of gray hair that had recently shown up.

My best friends had made a surprise visit to Kansas City with Robert being the mastermind behind it all. Upon first seeing each other, we cried, sang, and clapped 'The Makidada' from the movie, *The Color Purple*.

After gathering ourselves, I walked over to him, hugged him, kissed him gently on the lips, and whispered, "I'll thank you later."

He smiled and said, "Happy Birthday, baby. Enjoy your girls. Enjoy your weekend."

Rob sensed how this new and different city change was affecting me. At times, I enjoyed Kansas City with its big town spirit and classy, friendly people while in other times, I felt a sense of loneliness and disconnect, yet continued with a smile. An Orlando, Esther Rolle moment or something that felt like home was needed. My Orlando best friends were the remedy as we shopped, ate and stayed up all night reminiscing about the past and sharing our present status, which could not be done during my wedding's events. Their presence was just 'what the doctor ordered,' making it the best birthday ever.

I married a 'Mama's boy.' This was recognized early on in our relationship. In having dated Rob for only a month, he asked me to meet his mother, Willa, who was visiting him there in Atlanta.

In sharing the news with one of my best friends, who would be my maid of honor, she responded, "Annie, isn't it too soon to meet his mama?"

I responded, "No, not with this dude. It's nothing special about me meeting her. I got a feeling he's introduced every girlfriend to his mama."

It was later confirmed that my suspicion was correct. In regards to his mother, Robert was very loving and caring, being very attentive to her needs and always in good, respectful communication.

They say, "Watch how a man treats his mother! If he treats his mother well, he will treat his wife just the same." If the saying is true, I was in good hands.

They also say, "Mothers of 'mama's boys' will get in their son's marriage and cause issues."

Thankfully, Willa Shaw wasn't like that. As far as I was concerned, she was kind and respectful of our marriage. If Willa knew or was told anything, she discreetly kept it to herself not exposing it in our interactions. There was much appreciation for that. She would call before a visit, and ask if she could cook something for dinner when hearing that I had a late night on the job.

Our relationship was cordial, however, on the periphery, as our mother-in-law/daughter-in-law relationship had not yet bonded. This would soon change as we were to take our first trip together to Albuquerque, New Mexico for a Women's Prayer Conference. It was organized by the regional Bishop's wife/Supervisor whom we affectionately called Rev. "C." As a visionary, she organized many spiritual women conferences around the world; however, this would be the first one Willa and I would attend so we were very excited. While in Albuquerque, we enjoyed going to the various seminars, sightseeing and in our down time, we would sit in the hotel room and just talk.

One afternoon, our conversation took a turn as led by me. "You know I've been feeling maternal for the past few months. I'm ready to be a mom."

Her eyes lit up as the subject matter piqued her interest.

She was already a doting grandmother of twins and was amazing in this role. Often, I watched her horseplay with them, buy them every cute outfit in the store, and cook whatever food that they thought they wanted. She was one of *those* grandmothers and with another grandchild added to her brood, this would excitedly put her over the top. In continuing the conversation, I told her about the earlier false alarm in thinking I was pregnant only to have hopes shattered. At this point, I had only shared this emotion with Robert and my mother. By allowing my mother-in-law to know my inner self, it served as a big step in our relationship. She was empathetic and encouraging as she told me to keep the faith.

During this prayer convocation, my mother-in-law and I attended a session entitled 'Miracle at Midnight' that was led by a guest female bishop from Arizona along with other prophetesses. The spiritual fervor was high as the bishop and others began to minister powerfully and prophetically throughout the room.

One of the prophetesses said, "There are women here who want to conceive but have not yet. Come and we will pray over you."

One by one, various women came forward. My mother-in-law and I looked in disbelief at each other.

Willa whispered, "Ann, it's your time. Why don't you go up?"

Nervously, I responded in faith by making my way to the front of the room.

My hands were lifted high as prayers were spoken over me even those in unknown tongues. Before I knew it, I was 'slain in the spirit,' which is a term that is used to describe a faint that is caused by the overwhelming power of the Holy Spirit.

When I awoke, the prophetess declared, "She will be here in nine months!"

My mother-in-law and I left that women's conference in awe of what we both saw and experienced. After returning home, I shared it all with Robert, especially the part about *her arriving in nine months*. Admittedly, there were doubts and questions. Did she prophesy or "prophe-lie?" "But if it is from God, you will not be able to stop them," it says in the good book from Acts 5:39. Time will tell. Time will tell.

Strong ROOTS

The African Methodist Episcopal (AME) Church is the oldest black denomination in the world being founded in 1787 by our first Bishop, Richard Allen. It started as a protest when Richard Allen, Absalom Jones and others walked out of St. George Methodist Church in Philadelphia because they were told that they could not pray in the same altar section as the white congregants. With slavery being prevalent at the time, Allen and others like the characters in the television series, *Alex Haley's ROOTS*, refused to be called or treated anything less than a child of God. *Black lives matter*, so that Sunday, they left St. George, went across the street to a blacksmith shop and that's where the African Methodist Episcopal Church began.

As a child, the importance of our Methodist history was engrained in us by our parents. It was even evident at St. Mark's parsonage. When persons entered the living room, they were greeted by two 16 x 20 portrait wall hangings. One of the portraits carried the face of Richard Allen and the other portrait carried John Wesley, the father of Methodism.

There were many famous persons who have been connected with the denomination including the Mother of Civil Rights, Rosa Parks, Rev. Oliver Brown, the AME pastor in whom the landmark Brown vs. Board of Education Civil Lawsuit was named, and Esther Rolle. The African Methodist Episcopal (AME) Church is the denomination in which I am ordained as earlier generations of Father including my great-great-uncles, Reverends DS, Elijah, and Elisha Saunders, who were Morris

Brown University graduates in the 1930s and pastored in north Georgia. Earlier generations of Mother were as well.

Every four years, the AME Church convenes for the General Conference. This Conference is exceptional from other conferences for it is the place where Delegates, Alternates, and Observers from all over the world gather to vote on legislation and to elect Connectional Officers, General Officers and Bishops, which is the highest office in the church.

My parents brought me and my siblings to our first General Conference in 1980 when it was in New Orleans, LA, only months after our Esther Rolle visit. We stayed at the Le Pavillon Hotel, whose name was hard for us to pronounce due to to its French etymology. We were jaw dropped in being greeted by massive sculptures as we entered the lobby. In awe, we took in its presence along with the majestic Bishops purple robes who had gathered along with thousands of other AMEs in the convention space near the SuperDome. George followed Father around while Tymy and I stayed close with Mother. This General Conference was quite memorable as others later would be.

The General Conference of 2004 would prove to be the most significant for the Champions as AMEs descended upon Indianapolis, IN. This July, Robert and I were excited as I was two months pregnant, which fell in sync with the prophetess timeline from the prayer convocation. Father was optimistic as he had aspirations of being elected bishop, believing that his extensive resumé including having served twelve years as a general officer in the position of Worship and Evangelism Director would help him get there.

Mother was counted in this General Conference number too and was excited but for different reasons, as she had not been to one since 1980. Even in 1992, with the General Conference being in her own backyard, Orlando, FL, Mother expressed sadness in not being able to attend due to work responsibilities. However, her heart was always with the AME Church, as she would often reminisce of church stories in the past and express her joy in hosting church dignitaries and their families at St. Mark's parsonage. Mother was a granddaughter of an AME pastor, Rev. George Washington Hartage, who helped build rural Samuel Chapel AME Church, Buena Vista, GA, a place where she had fond childhood memories. She also treasured the AME relationships that she had formed through her adult years and was elated that her pastor from St. Mark was running for bishop. She was totally committed in campaigning for him to get him elected.

Robert and I thought it would be a good time to tell both of them that they were going to be grandparents. When bearing the baby news, they both were overjoyed as well as other close friends whom we told. The General Conference was more than a slate of legislation, election, and a voting apparatus. It was also a family reunion, where it was a reuniting of friends from all over the world, some of whom had not seen each other since the last General Conference. Over the years, I enjoyed watching Father reunite with other ministers here, especially his roommates from seminary. One of them, being a popular, fair-skinned civil rights pastor from upstate New York who always smoked a pipe, while another was a dark-skinned, fiery, popular pastor from Alabama. Whenever they saw each other, they were all jovial in spirit, child-like in reminiscence of their seminary days as they kept referring to father as "Champ." This General Conference, however, they were all running for the office of 'Bishop,' which meant competition. It didn't matter in this moment. They were able to put their political differences aside and just be friends.

The campaign journey for any elected office is serious business as was the case at this General Conference. There were campaign songs, give-a-ways, and creative licensing, like persons walking on stilts with signage endorsing their candidate. Father even had a group of young men from Eatonville, FL mime to the song "You're Next in Line for a Miracle" by Marvin Sapp. Their anointed ministry drew a big crowd.

It was an interesting dichotomy between the Champions this General Conference. While George and I would help with Father's campaign booth, Mother worked feverishly at her pastor's campaign booth. Whenever there was any free time, we would go check on Mother as she always said that she was fine, but 'fine' was an understatement. Mother was in her element as we witnessed her hug and converse with strangers as well as acquaintances from the Women's Missionary Society also known as the WMS, a women's organization in the AME Church that focused on advancing global missions through economic, social, and educational development. Some of these persons she had not seen in years, yet Mother kept her mission focused on the importance of encouraging others to vote for her pastor.

Not only being optimistic about himself getting elected, Father also spoke highly of other candidates whom he thought would make a good Bishop as well. The Day of the Election had come. There were seven (7) bishopric candidates elected that year. The Pastor of the "Jesus Saves" Church that I attended in

Atlanta would be one of them as well as Mother's pastor of St. Mark Church, Orlando, FL. Father would fall short.

When the family returned to his hotel suite, there was a cold silence in the air. Father went to the restroom yet left the door cracked where I could see his silhouette. Making my way in, I offered condolences as Father leaned over the sink with pain on his face. Soon after, his cell phone rang. When Father answered, I overheard the voice of another bishopric candidate who too didn't get elected. It was a grief support session as they expressed their disappointments.

The candidate who called Father asked, "What am I going to do now Champ?"

Father responded, "What are you going to do? You're going to go back to your church, love the people and be the best pastor they ever had! That's what you're going to do!"

Father had a way of encouraging others even when he was distressed. He was just that kind of man.

When a candidate is not elected, it not only affects the candidate but it affects the family as well. George was there as he was helping out with conference security. Soon after the election, we both connected and expressed great grief with Father's non-election. After seeing George, I ran into Mother who was coming down the hall in a green blazer along with a couple of other St. Mark members, including her pastor's sister and dear friend. They looked as though they were coming from a victory party. The word 'ecstatic' would describe their behavior as should any family member or friend of a candidate who is elected. Many tireless nights, hard work, energy, and effort goes on behind the scenes to make that moment happen. Leaving the booth, I greeted them all and offered "Congratulations." They soon left as I was standing there just with Mother.

In trying to cover up my feelings, I said, "Congratulations Mama! You all did it! Your pastor is now a Bishop... well-deserved."

She sensed my pain of Father's defeat as a good mother would. Mother looked at me and offered sympathy. "I'm sorry your father didn't make it baby... I really am."

We hugged as I cried in her arms like a baby. Though the cry was for Father, nobody could comfort me in that moment like Mother, nobody.

In returning home, life eventually went back to normal but the effects from the General Conference still lingered, especially with Father. He eventually returned to the pastorate but it wasn't like St. Mark, no 'Esther Rolle' moments, just grief over what could've been, with uncertainty of what would happen to his ministerial career. During this time, family even encouraged him to pursue writing again. Father always said he wanted to write a novel on the life of Henry McNeil Turner, who was not only a bishop in the AME Church but was also a successful reconstruction era politician. He declined as his love for writing seemed to diminish during his bereavement period.

Digesting SOUL FOOD

Four days after celebrating our daughter's third birthday, we welcomed our son into the world. With already having a daughter, Rob and I were excited to now have a son as demonstrated in the doctor's office with hollers and high-fives upon first hearing the news. He had finally arrived. We had another apple on the Champion/Shaw family tree. Our parents were more than ecstatic, with my mother-in-law even trading in her car for a bigger one to hold all four of her grandbabies comfortably. My parents were rearranging work and meeting times as I had to ensure proper scheduling so that each had a quality Kansas City visitation. This kind of family time management is necessary when you have divorced parents.

Mother was the first to arrive. Her caring smile and coifed curly hair was a constant in my life. She wore it well even in life's hardships, due to an understanding beautician/friend who offered a pay later plan. With Mother's keen eye and sense of time management in raising three children, her wisdom was most welcome in the adjustment to my second child. Mother always made herself useful on helping out in the kitchen, nursery, or wherever. She was happy as she enjoyed the company of her most precious gifts, her grandchildren.

Mother's visit, however, would go longer than expected due to a sudden event. We had just finished cooking breakfast when I beckoned for her to come and have breakfast. After walking in the bedroom to see what was wrong, she had a distant look, along with slow, slurred speech that came with a drooped mouth. We called 911 immediately in fear that she was suffering a stroke. After receiving a CAT-scan and multiple other tests, the doctors concluded that she had suffered a TIA, transient ischemic attack or a mini-stroke, and wanted to keep her in the hospital for a few days. My body was physically challenged as I walked down the long hospital halls to visit mother after recently giving birth and having my second caesarean. It was quite emotional seeing Mother in this fragile state. Up until this point, I had never known her to ever be in the hospital for any kind of sickness. Mother's illness would prolong her visit and things would grow more complex as Father was scheduled to soon arrive.

Father arrived at our home in his signature style with his long wool coat, dress pants, blazer, dress shirt, and beret. Rob had picked him up from the airport and had taken him by the hospital to have prayer for Mother, as it was father's request. When he walked in the door, we greeted one another but his main focus was on his grandchildren as he picked up his new grandson and immediately began to play with his granddaughter. My mother-in-love had come over to help prepare dinner, being that my second time mothering and hospital runs to see Mother were quite overwhelming. In what looked like a scene from the television series *Soul Food*, we sat down at the dining room table, offered prayer for Mother's healing and thanksgiving for our food.

Psychologists say that we marry men like our fathers but as far as I was concerned, this research didn't pertain to me. After all, Robert is dark complexion and Father is fair complexion. Robert is a member of a fraternity whose colors are black and gold and Father is a member of a different one whose colors are purple and gold.

Father took great pride in his fraternity, for on his left arm was a branded Omega Greek letter with the looks of a horseshoe. As a child first seeing it, I remember being in awe and asking Father for its meaning. "It means I'm an Omega man!" he would say boastfully. This fraternal boasting that I heard as a child would spill onto my adult dinner table as my husband and Father teased each other about their fraternal choices.

They would even use the Revelation biblical text where Jesus says, "I am the Alpha and the Omega, the First and the Last" in order to prove their fraternity's theological rank.

Robert would say, "Alpha was on God's mind, Dad! That's why he mentioned us first!"

Father would "clap" back. "Quite the contrary, son! God loved Omega so he saved the best for last!"

Father would then wink and everybody would laugh.

The dinner conversation, however, would prove that psychologists were indeed right as I sat and observed their similarities. Robert and Father's joke telling style was almost identical. They were both "mama's boys"; as Rob adored his mother so did Father adore his. Both fans of good preaching, they talked about their favorite preachers and sermons. Most of all, when it came to desserts, they both had a sweet tooth that could obsessively devour any baker's pound cake or peach cobbler, but not without ice cream.

Father would always have a racy response when asked if he wanted ice cream on his dessert. "Put a skirt on it!" he would say.

In the midst of babbling banter from this newfound "bromance," I found an entrance into the conversation.

"Are you ready for Good Friday, Daddy?" I asked Father.

"As ready as I'm going to be!" Father responded.

Father's visit was not just for his grandchildren but it was also due to a preaching invitation for the Seven Last Words Service. The 'Seven Last Words' is normally held on Good Friday where seven preachers will each preach one of the seven last words of Christ on the cross. Robert was also set to preach in the same Good Friday service.

Robert said, "Dad, you're preaching my favorite word, that seventh word. Father into thy hands, I commit my spirit."

Father responded, "No Robert, you're preaching my favorite word, that fourth word… 'Eli, Eli, lama sabachthani, My God, My God why have thou forsaken me?'"

There was a pregnant pause as Father put his elbow on the table while his hand rubbed his forehead—silent tears. His thoughts drifted far away as sometimes they would, especially since the last General Conference in not being elected a bishop.

To deflect the deafening silence, I interjected, "We can't forget that first word, my favorite. 'Father forgive them for they know not what they do.'"

"Oh yeah… that's a good one!" Rob and Father both said in agreement while offering relief for Father's scarred memory in bringing him back into the present moment.

Mother was released from the hospital on the morning of Good Friday. With Father's insistence, we were assured that he would carefully watch his grandbabies while we went to the hospital for her discharge. With a lap blanket on his shoulder, grandson in his arms, and his granddaughter, standing with one arm wrapped around his leg and fingers in her mouth, he proudly said, "We're good. After all, they're my grandchildren. I'll take care of them."

When we returned home, we placed Mother in the guest bedroom downstairs while inquiring about the quiet house. "They're sleep," Father said as he told us how he played a long game of 'Hide and Go Seek' with granddaughter, Raven, but was challenged with grandson's Robert, III, loud cries. "That boy is loud and his scrawls like a preacher but we came to an understanding!" Father said with a cunning smile as we all joined in laughter and agreeance. We talked but not for long as he and Robert had a Good Friday Service that they had to attend.

About an hour or so after they left, I received a phone call from my mother-in-love who had attended the Good Friday Service as well. "Listen… just listen." She held her cell phone out while I heard the voice of Father preaching the seventh last word. My heart rejoiced as the congregational responses affirmed the power that came from the pulpit.

When Father and Robert arrived home, they were giddy in sharing their commendations for each other's sermon. A couple of hours later, when returning upstairs to my bedroom suite, I discovered Father sitting on the olive green southern chaise mesmerized while watching the movie, *Amazing Grace*.

Amazing Grace is a story about the eighteenth century life of William Wilberforce, a British politician and his quest to abolish Great Britain's slave trade even in the midst of adversity.

It was not Father's first time watching *Amazing Grace* for he had seen it a couple of times before during his visit here. Like music, Father was a fan of movies having introduced me to classics like *Sounds of Music, King and I* during the summer of 1989 when I stayed with him in Jacksonville, FL. Father was always on top of his movie game and when he would discover one that touched his heart, like a beloved sermon or a song, he would put it on repeat, never faltering or wavering from it. This *Amazing Grace* would be no different so out of curiosity, I inquired of its sentiment. "Why do you like this movie so much?" I asked. Father went on to explain that he loved the movie because he could identify with William Wilberforce's belief in something so great that you never give up in accomplishing its goal. This ideology came with Father's decision to run again for Bishop in the AME Church, to much of the family's disagreement.

Our conversation soon shifted to other subject matters like politics, especially when it came to the presidential race. Though he was impressed with Barack Obama and his credentials, he didn't think America was ready to elect a black president.

"This country's not ready for that… one day, but not now," Father said.

Disagreeing with him, I reminded him of his political party.

"You wouldn't vote for him anyway, Republican," I jauntedly said.

"Yes, I would… I can vote for anyone I want to in the general election," he responded.

Immediately, I commented, "You voted for Ronald Reagan… remember Daddy?!"

With a smirk, he spoke of that moment where he along with his best friend attended Ronald Reagan's first inauguration in January 1981. Father even got a photo opportunity shaking the hand of then Vice President George Bush which was a picture that he proudly displayed on the tall chest of drawers in the St. Mark Parsonage. In a minority class, as a registered African American Republican, Father believed that the African American voice should not be one dimensional, beholden to one particular political party but should have representation in other political parties as well.

After a round of political punditry, we spoke about persons and events of our past. There was even mention of Brett, the houseguest from Jacksonville, FL who was kicked out of the house for relapsing on crack. Father now spoke fondly of him, "He's doing great now! He's remarried, rebuilt his career, and has left those drugs alone for good!" Brett wasn't the only one doing great, for Father appeared to be emotionally doing much better and Mother's physical health was steadily improving.

One morning while in the kitchen, our attention would turn to my siblings as Father mentioned spending time with Tymy. "I need to get back to Orlando so I can have my weekly dinner with your sister," Father commented. By now, Tymy was living in Orlando with Mother, but Father would take Tymy out every Saturday for their daddy-daughter date nights. He then looked out the window and said, "I worry about my son, George." As a concerned Father for his son, he exhaled and went into deep thought. At this point, George's education was limited not yet having a college degree, and his work wasn't constant leaving us to wonder about his economic status. George's movements were mysterious. We knew he lived in Atlanta, had a church affiliation but people, even family, only tell what they want you to know.

"Don't worry, Daddy," I told Father. "George will be alright. He's a survivor. He will be alright."

"You think so?" Father replied.

"Yeah… Yeah," I said as I shook my head up and down.

Father then agreed and followed suit in gesture.

Father eventually left for Orlando as Mother would leave about a week or so later. After my parents' visitation, my spring cleaning mode set in with determination to clean the house from top to bottom. The children's godparents picked them up for an outing which freed me from any interruptions in getting the job done. At the end of the cleaning episode, there was a feeling of renewal and the day would end with a hot bubble bath as an award for my accomplishment. The children soon arrived sound asleep having already taken their baths and dressed in pajamas. There was a spirit of peace that filled the atmosphere and a comfort that called from my bed as it awaited my presence. It was the calm before the storm.

On April 20, 2008, 5:00 a.m., the house phone rang. It had actually rang earlier but due to our lethargy and deep sleep, we were unresponsive. Robert sluggishly got out of bed and answered the phone then belted out an "Oh no." After hanging up, he walked over to my bedside.

"What's wrong with the family?" I said.

"Come with me, baby, we got to talk," he said calmly as he led me over to the southern chaise.

After sitting, he nervously said, "Dad suffered a heart attack last night."

In surprise, I shouted, "What?! We've got to pack up and go and make sure he's alright!"

Rob slightly turned his head as if to say no while deeply gazing into my eyes to make the emotional connection that his mouth could never articulate.

Father was dead.

A shout of shock would come from my loins as Rob offered condolences while the sounds of the Florida Mass Choir singing "Storms Clouds Rising" would prophetically speak to me as it played through the cable music television station from our armoire.

Robert would attend church that Sunday but didn't get far in leading worship as he was so overwhelmed with grief that my brother-in-law, Bryan, and a church officer would assist him in service responsibilities. There would be no public worship for me as my church service would be in my bedroom with a pool of tears and a repetitive prayer of "Why Lord?!? Why?!?" My mother-in-love would hold down the fort in caring for the children and intercepting condolence calls that came from all over the country. All were heavy, hearteningly surprised that "Champ is gone." Grief makes one weak but later that afternoon,

I gathered enough strength to greet pastoral friends who stopped by for a bereavement visit.

Years earlier, in 1989, Father was in a tragic car accident. His car was obliterated yet he only acquired minimal scarring. "It's a miracle that he's alive!" the doctors declared. There were tears of joy as Father was given another chance of life. This event, however, would not end with a miracle like the one before. There would be no valiant return or quick comeback from this massive heart attack. It would end with death and endless tears of sorrow.

The flight from Kansas City to Orlando was long and dreary. Along with looking through old photo albums, I attempted to recover my last memories of Father alive. The last morning that I saw him, his breakfast included a sausage burrito from the nearest fast food restaurant. Father was dressed in a navy blue blazer, white dressed shirt, tan dress slacks before dashing out to the airport with Robert. There were even more recent memories of talking with him on the phone numerous times including our last conversation in which he still expressed excitement over our last visit. Father was even adamant about talking with his three-year-old granddaughter, Raven, who he called his namesake being that they shared the middle name 'Lovelace.' This phone conversation took place on a Friday.

Father had a hacking, dry cough that kept our call brief but he made me a promise. "I'll go to the doctor on Monday."

God had other plans. Sunday came. Father died. Now, I was on the way to his funeral.

George would meet me in Orlando having driven from Atlanta.

"Sis! I don't believe this! I can't believe Daddy is gone!" he exclaimed.

"I know Bro! I know how you feel! I can't either!" I responded.

In inquiring with Tymy about her feelings, she didn't say much but her demeanor was very sad and distant.

We were so grieved until we opted out of seeing Father's body for the family viewing. We decided to wait until the visitation to see the 'unbelievable' as we were experiencing traumatic grief that is triggered when a loved one dies suddenly.

The visitation services for Father would not be at St. Mark; instead, it was at another AME Church across town. Upon entering the vestibule with George, Tymy, Robert, and our children, we all tried to prepare ourselves for what we would witness. Emotional, I stopped before entering the sanctuary doors to gather myself.

A familiar woman immediately came toward me and said, "Are you alright?"

For a moment, I looked at her and thought, Hell Naw! I'm not alright! My daddy is dead!

People can say some stupid sh** to the newly mourned.

The "Are you alright?" line is the worst.

An "I'm sorry for your loss" or "You're in our prayers" will suffice.

After her comment, I gestured with my head and hand as if to say "I'm good."

I wasn't good though. Father's death had sent me in a shock. As we made our way around the casket, I barely looked inside only glanced. Afterwards, I turned my face away being spared of the details. Holding on to more than just Robert's hand, I was holding God's unchanging hand really tight for God was the only one who could keep me.

The next day, as we processed in for the funeral, there was a surreal feeling that overshadowed me as we solemnly walked down the aisle of St. Mark. There were countless familiar and foreign faces who greeted us. Some, who were there with Father's ministry, which included the Esther Rolle moment, came to say goodbye. Most of the family managed to get through the funeral service in one piece but for me, the most difficult part was leaving the cemetery with Father's casket still sitting above ground. In walking away, a part of me was left behind with him.

This "foggy" feeling would follow me after the funeral as I exchanged my hospice job for a new one as a pediatric hospital chaplain in Kansas City, MO. In working the graveyard shift, four nights a week, my presence and counsel was needed mostly for the parents not for the children. In this line of ministry, I discovered that most children have a certain resiliency where they are able to emotionally handle health issues far better than adults. Between comforting parents and families in the loss of premature babies or even rejoicing in the recovery of others, I would retreat to my small office in the lower level of the hospital. It was my crying chamber in mulling over Father's obituary as I went through every detail and stared at every picture. Father's body was gone and only memories remained, so I held them close in mind and spirit.

In July of 2008, there would only be one named Champion who would be at the General Conference in St. Louis, Missouri—me. In as many years, far back as I could remember, the Champion family would be represented in numbers.

In speaking with George a month earlier, I inquired about his attendance. He responded, "You know I'm not going to that!"

One of my favorite aunts whom I could readily depend on to be at other General Conferences responded, "That's it for me niece."

With Father being gone, things just weren't the same for any of us. We could always depend on seeing Father at the General Conference, so our attendance just three months after his death was too much handle.

With strength from God, I attended the opening worship service. When the congregation began to sing the hymn "And Are We Yet Alive?" I almost lost it. This hymn was sang traditionally at the opening worship of every General Conference but this year I wasn't ready to hear it. "And are we yet alive?" My internal response to the question. No. We're not all alive. My father is dead. In observing the retired General Officers section, my thoughts fell on Father. If he was alive, he woud've been standing there with the rest of them. In remembrance, Father sang this song with movement and fervor at past General Conferences. He was alive then but he's dead now. In the middle of the song, I sat down in feeling as though the breath was leaving my body as I continued to grapple with Father's untimely death. On the edge of an anxiety attack, I said a prayer and pondered on my favorite scripture to gain composure.

"Do not be anxious about anything, but in every situation, by prayer and petition, with thanksgiving, present your requests to God. And the peace of God, which transcends all understanding, will guard your hearts and your minds in Christ Jesus." Philippians 4:6-8

After managing to get through the worship service, I left the General Conference with my children, leaving Robert behind to handle his delegation duties.

Grief doesn't go away. It lingers. No matter where you go or what you do, it has a tendency to hang around and even find itself in unlikely places. One day, I was in the cleaners waiting in line to drop off my clothes when I overheard familiar music from the intercom. It was Neil Diamond's "Hello Again," which was one of Father's favorite songs. The remembrance of him playing Neil Diamond's cassette tape in that Lincoln Towncar while driving and singing along was too vivid of a memory. I got out of there like the speed of lightning before my pain was exposed.

Later that year, I reflected on one of my last conversations with Father where he didn't believe America was ready to elect a black president because of its issues with racism. America would prove him wrong. In November of that year , Barack Hussein Obama was elected the 44th President of the United States of America. Robert and I were blessed to be two of the almost 2 million who in the freezing cold would witness this historical Presidential Inauguration. As we stood, I was emotional as I thought of Father who was there on the same grounds 28 years earlier for a different political party and a different president.

Father once told me, "I don't want to die of Alzheimer's… when it's my time, I want to go in my right mind." God gave him his desire. The writer August Wilson wrote, "You die how you live." Father lived life fast and full, spending most of his time in doing the good work of helping others. He was also a very prideful man who did not want his family to see him suffering. With this knowledge, it caused some relief but there was still the uncertainty of his wellbeing before he left this Earth. Was he disheartened? Was he at peace? In grappling with these issues, there were sleepless nights. Furthermore, being that Father had announced prior to his death that he would run again for Bishop, I wondered about the challenges that he faced in deciding to do so.

My answer would come in a dream where Father and I stood on the sideline while watching persons campaign at a General Conference. Father was dressed in his blazer, turtleneck sweater, and dress pants.

As we watched, I asked Father, "Are you alright?"

He looked at me with a smile and responded peacefully "I'm alright baby… don't worry about me. I'm alright!"

It was a gift of grace to have that dream in that it gave me peace to know that Father was just as he told me, 'Alright.'

Me and Robert's tenure at our first church would soon end and our time in Kansas City was over, at least for awhile. We were now headed to St. Louis and only God knew what awaited us there.

Hey THAT'S MY MAMA

Though they both reside in the same state, St. Louis is quite different from Kansas City, being twice its size. St. Louis, known for the Gateway Arch, has Southern remnants with an East Coast tapestry where Kansas City is Mid-West from its culture to its geographical landscape. Instead of hearty beef and bar-b-que from Kansas City, St. Louis now greeted us with tasty toasted ravioli and gooey butter cake. To top it off, St. Louis, was the name of the city and the county which had a plethora of municipalities. There were 88 to be exact, including one named Beverly Hills, MO with a population of 574.

We were now at a different congregation in St. Louis that was located on a popular street called Kingshighway. With each new church, there was a new nickname. This derived from Robert's marketing background in hopes to promote the church in a more contemporary fashion. With our first church in Kansas City, its nickname was the A-TEAM with the A standing for 'Allen' signifying the last name of the AME Church's founder, Richard Allen. Its inspiration, however, came from the 80's hit television show *The A-Team*, starring Mr. T. With the St. Louis church, its nickname would be the J-C.R.E.W. whose acronym stood for "Jesus Christ Reigns and Everybody Wins." Its nickname was inspired by the fashion store who offered classic styles for young people.

This was appropriate because the J-C.R.E.W. was a more youthful congregation than our first one in Kansas City. Demographically, the congregation wasn't just younger in age but also in spirit as evident by the main mother of the church who was a widow and former church first lady. In her 80s, she not only cooked most of the church's dinners but still wore 4-inch heels, fashionable clothes, and with sass used the word 'girlfriend' in her casual conversations. The congregation was very interactive especially in the preaching moment, and whenever the main mother of the church liked what she heard, she would holla, "Deal with it!"

Rob and I would deal with it in this new life of being in a new city. We had now exchanged our 4-bedroom parsonage for a 2-bedroom apartment. We were grateful that our children were too small to know the difference as they now shared a bedroom. As a two-income household, the job hunt was another priority. Thankfully, I would eventually land another chaplain position with a wonderful hospice organization. Change happens quickly so we had to familiarize ourselves with our new surroundings and find a new pre-school, new grocery store, new cleaners, new hairdresser, and the other 'news' that comes with moving to a different city.

In February of that year, however, we would experience something very familiar. While on the way to my son's first birthday party, I would get a call. It was a member from St. Mark informing me that Mother was in the hospital from an apparent 'blackout' at a grocery store. Instead of being fully engaged with my son on his big day, my concern was on Mother as Robert and I researched last-minute airline tickets to Orlando, FL so that I could be at Mom's bedside.

During that year, there were three emergency trips from St. Louis to Orlando that centered around Mother and health issues, with the third trip being longer than the ones before due to Mother's extended hospitalization. After countless tests and x-rays, the diagnosis was pronounced as early stage Parkinson's disease whose symptoms include tremor in one hand along with slow movement, stiffness, and balance loss. Decisions had to be made not just for Mother but for Tymy, who with special needs was placed under Mother's care. Housing arrangements would be made for Tymy while George and I would have ongoing conversations about Mother's status. Ultimately, the responsibility of Mother's long-term plan of care would eventually lie with Robert and myself as we faced the reality that she was no longer able to function as head of her household.

It was a difficult conversation in trying to convince Mother that it was time for her to move to St. Louis with us. She eventually yielded in knowing that ultimately, it was best for her. After Mother agreed, she gave her list of keepsakes, and emphatically said, "Please don't throw away any of my pictures! They will be worth something one day!" Family was supportive, including my uncle and aunt who came from Jacksonville, Florida to help me pack. We would remember Mother's plea as we made transition.

As we packed, I noticed how the inside of the home looked almost exactly the way it did when I left home for college twenty years earlier. It was the same borrowed furniture, and mix-matched chairs around the dining room table. The piano brought back memories of Tymy playing Clementi's Sonatina in C Major, Opus 36 as well as us trying to tickle the keys of Linus and Lucy, Peanuts theme song. It was the same piano that we had in the parsonage during our Esther Rolle moment.

In my old bedroom, there on the wall was my high school choral medals, and a picture of the 1990-91 Jones High School football team who was runner-up in the state championship. On my dresser, there was an old brown, radio clock that used to belt the 80's Rock and R&B hits of the day. As I walked over to the bedroom window and peered through the olive green curtain that was held together by a clothes pin, the presence of the black rod iron window gate was a reminder of that horrific event that caused it to be there in the first place. Mother liberated me from that window gate and the walls of pain that it represented.

In the television sitcom *That's My Mama*, the widowed mother's main focus was ensuring that her son settled down and lived a good productive life. Mother's desire was the same for me as now, I was set off on my journey in being an ordained minister, healthcare chaplain, married, and a mother of two young children living slap dab in the middle of America, Missouri. At the time, Mother set me free, I never thought about her joining me this soon in hopes that her health would stay strong but life comes with unpredictability. Her life was changing which meant ours was as well.

Friends and neighbors were informed of Mother's move including my god sister and her parents who lived across the street and regularly came to check on Mother and Tymy. The hardest departure of all was saying good-bye to St. Mark. On the last Sunday in August 2010, after being a member there for over 40 years, Mother gave her emotional good-bye speech and we were headed off, pictures and all.

A month earlier, in St. Louis, we had moved from a two-bedroom apartment to a now three-bedroom home in LaDue

County, known for its great public school system as it would work well for our oldest daughter, Raven who, at the time was a budding kindergartener. We had a more spacious house as it was our intent for our children to finally have their own bedrooms. This would be a dream deferred with mother's relocation but with godly gratitude that our children were not of age where they would be repelled by staying in the same bedroom, once again. A few months later, Tymy would join us in St. Louis and my hospice co-worker, a jovial and kind social worker, would assist me in getting her placed in a special home.

In a matter of short time, our St. Louis Family had now grown from four persons to six as we were thankful that our tan navigator was able to carry us all to church. We were now in two worlds somewhere between pediatric and geriatric appointments. At times, it was hard trying to keep up with a two-year-old energetic toddler and a five-year-old bright kindergartener while slowing down for a 72-year-old maturing mother. It was official as Rob and I were now apart of the sandwich generation, which is a generation of people primarily in their 30s or 40s, who are responsible for raising their children and caring for aging parents.

We tried to make things comfortable for Mother while including her in church activities, especially those in which she was familiar, like the Women's Missionary Society. Mother was even excited to attend the Joy and Jazz Event that the church sponsored. Being dressed in purple, Mother seemed to gleam the entire night as she took in the ambience and the company of her new church family.

After the first year of residing with us, Mother's aging process unfolded right in front of our eyes. She repetitively enjoyed sharing old family stories and pictures of her grandparents. There was one in particular, her paternal grandmother named Annie Pearl Park White, half black and half Caucasian, who she often spoke of in saying that she passed away at their Ellaville, Georgia childhood home. At night, Mother would part her hair in the center and braid each side, baring a striking resemblance to great-grandmother Annie Pearl. Mother would then gently nod off in her chair.

Although she enjoyed her grandchildren most of the time, there were other times when there was a sense of agitation in sharing personal space with four other persons. Mother was even challenged in having to now endure sub-zero climate of St. Louis's winter weather. Her homesickness was increasingly telling as she had "Georgia on her mind" in often speaking about her family who lived there. We had to do something about it.

In December of 2011, Mother was in holiday cheer as we made our way to the St. Louis Airport. She was going home to Georgia. The memory of that morning is vivid as I escorted her through the airport in a wheelchair. Prior to arriving at her gate, we would get a cup of coffee and then talk before boarding her plane. Mother was the happiest in spirit and cognitively clear as she talked about her future plans of Georgia visits that included her high school where she was the class queen and salutatorian. Before leaving each other's presence, our hug had an unusual strength and comfort unlike the ones before, as we then waved with her being escorted into the airplane tunnel.

On New Year's Day of the next year, while enjoying a family dinner with black eyed peas and plenty of good laughs, I would get a phone call from George informing me that Mother suffered a stroke. Struggling to hold my composure, I was back on a plane for another hospital visit but this time in another city, Atlanta. Thoughts and questions raced in my mind as I couldn't believe that Mother's health was in such a poor state. When I arrived at the hospital, she was in ICU and non-responsive.

After a week of no changes, the doctors offered a grim report. Fear, anxiety, and selfishness arose as I wasn't ready to lose my mother. The truth of the matter is I wasn't over the loss of Father as I still grieved him almost four years after his passing. The thought of Mother being gone from me was too much. Needing her with me, I wasn't ready for her to go. In my prayers, while holding the bar rails on Mother's hospital bed, I hollered to heaven for Mother's recovery. God granted favor and Mother became responsive; however, she wasn't the same as before. She was now non-ambulatory, cognition minimal and her speech was confined to mere mumbles. After hospitalization discharge, she was admitted to a skilled nursing facility there in Atlanta.

For the next few months, I would travel back and forth to Atlanta in checking on Mother. Still, I maintained my duties as wife, mother, asst. pastor, and hospice chaplain. After almost a year at the Atlanta skilled nursing facility, we had Mother transferred to a more reputable, patient-attentive, skilled facility in St. Louis where a few of my hospice patients resided. While there, after visiting with patients, I would visit Mother often as she either lay in bed or sat up in a wheelchair, wordless but still bearing a strong presence.

Troubled waters hit home, which sometimes happens in marriages, as Robert and I had a purging of the souls. Hurt and betrayal was discovered as our marriage was now on the fringes. Like our wedding ceremony in the "Jesus Saves" Church, it was hard trying to remain cool in an extremely hot atsmosphere of pain. The emotions of my failing marriage weighed heavy in my soul though I attempted to publicly conceal it with smiles and cordiality.

That summer, I even traveled to Washington, DC, with thousands of other sorority members to celebrate our 100th year celebration. My "Delta aunts," who were my inspiration for joining our sorority, were in on the fun. It was a great getaway from my home situation. It felt great to be around the love and energy that is constant during our national conventions.

One of the events at the 100th year Celebration National Convention was our ecumenical service. At the conclusion of our ecumenical service, our national chaplain called for the sorority chaplains, like myself, to lead persons in prayer. As each soror, the name given to a woman who is of the same sorority, came to my prayer line, their request was centered around forgiveness and marriage in some form or fashion. What were the odds? Out of all the thousands of sorors that attended that service, these unacquainted, divine 'select,' would come through my prayer line grappling with the same issue of 'forgiveness' as myself. God does nothing by chance but by design. Not only was there a stronger bond with my sorority, there was a keener awareness that I was not alone in my pain. The words from

Father, "Forgiveness is the most important word in marriage," echoed in my spirit as I left the Convention.

Back in St. Louis, I had a support system who were prayer warriors, seasoned women in ministry with wise counsel and godly connection concerning my situation. There was also a remembrance of Mother, who before my 'hot' wedding ceremony would offer words of advice.

"Marriage is beautiful but it can be hard. Never rush to make a big decision based off of emotion no matter what the situation. Always pray and wait for an answer. Know that I will always be praying for you." Mother's words resounded as I was grappling with my place of marital conflict.

Finding my way at her bedside, I spoke to her reminding her of those words she said to me.

With tears coming down my cheek, I asked, "Mama are you still praying for me?"

Soon after, though her eyes were fixated on the wall, I felt a touch of her hand cover my own. Her gentle and strong touch that was reassuring in my hurts as a child would now comfort my wounded spirit as a woman. It was a sign that even though her speech was stricken, the prayers would still ascend through the heart.

Marital reconciliation soon followed. Our first wedding gift, the book, *Single, Married, Separated, and Life after Divorce* ministered in a powerful way. Counseling and fervent prayer was now in progress. Even Luther Vandross's music re-entered our lives, just as the cool Bishop at our wedding encouraged us to do so. All of these measures helped to get our marriage back on track.

A year or so later, my family would find themselves in Kansas City, Missouri once again. Our new church was red brick with a beautiful sanctuary that was built over a hundred years ago by its members. It was located in the vine district of the city. We would nickname this church "THE BETHEL LIGHT" as this congregation exuded a hospitable and caring spirit.

Our residence was located in North Kansas City as Mother's nursing facility was only ten minutes away. During the week, I would often visit Mother at any given time, showing up with the staff unaware to make sure that they were rightly offering Mother good quality care. One Tuesday, while having dinner with my family before the children's music lessons, I had a peculiar feeling that I needed to check on Mother immediately. When I walked in her room, her eyes were closed and her complexion had a 'grayish' tone. When trying to awaken her, it looked as though her eyes had rolled to the back of her head. Immediately, I called for the nurse and demanded that she call 911.

After being at the hospital all night, I went home to prepare for work as I was to arrive around 8:30 a.m. By now, I was employed at a hospital in North Kansas City which was the same hospital where Mother had been admitted. As a member of the Supportive Care Team, we counseled patients and families on their healthcare options when there has been a change in the patient's health status. The team consisted of a Palliative Care physician, registered nurses, social workers, and myself, the chaplain. During our morning briefings, each team member would give the status of each patient on the supportive care list. After the physician asked for referrals, I offered.

"Yes, I have a referral." Speaking with slowness and intentionality while trying to contain my tears, I continued, "My mother, she was admitted last night."

The team looked surprised and concerned as I explained my insomnia and the turn of Mother's health events. Her status had now changed as she had suffered yet another stroke.

We soon scheduled a supportive care team meeting where instead of being the caregiver, I was now the 'cared for.' Instead of being the provider, I was now the recipient. Mother's healthcare directive listed me as the DPOA, Durable Power of Attorney, where my job was to ensure that her desires were implemented. It was a hard seat to sit in but it comes a time in all of our lives where we have to sit down and make the hard decisions, especially when it comes to our loved ones. Prior to her stroke, Mother stated her healthcare wishes. She was eventually admitted to the Hospice House that was located in the hospital.

For about ten days, either myself, Robert, or other family and friends were at bedside making sure she was well attended. We even contacted aunts and uncles who were out of town making sure that Mother heard their voice. George soon came in from Atlanta, emotional in hopes that things would turn around and Mother, like always, would recover.

Prayers and words of love poured over her while gospel music continually filled the atmosphere ministering to her faith. As apnea settled in, Mother's earthly time was coming to an end. When death is imminent, some persons desire family and friends to lay witness as they take their last breath while others desire a more private and peaceful passing in leaving the world with only the Divine present. Knowing Mother, the latter would be her choice. Her sacred space was offered. Seven minutes after leaving Mother's room, I received a call that she was gone.

Sometime afterward, we called to inform George of the news, and he was devastated. We then brought Tymy, who had relocated to Kansas City with us, to Mother's bedside and informed her of Mother's death. Her response was a "Oh no!" with a facial look of sheer horror that seemed to last momentarily. There were no tears only a myriad of questions. Tymy rarely showed outward displays of emotion. Even when Father died, I never saw her cry in response, never.

My grief was heavy as a mother's death is different from any other. It followed me, even on Sunday morning, as our Kansas City 'Bethel Light' congregation was very supportive. After worship, a group of women who also lost their mothers would greet me and offer their condolences. In that sacred space of 'motherless' women, there was no preacher and parishioner, no religious hierarchy, we were all just sisters, equals, who knew this kind of pain. In that moment, I found comfort with their words and hugs. They say "losing your mother is like losing your best friend." This sadness was overhelming as I wanted to hang my head down in defeat. It was Mother's words of always telling me to keep my head up that prompted me not to do such a thing.

When you're the responsible party of the deceased, your grief is sidelined with funeral business. It was always Mother's desire for her funeral services to be held in Orlando at St. Mark. Though Ellaville, GA was her demographical home, Orlando, Florida, and more particularly St. Mark, was her 'heart' home.

It was the place of her greatest memories and her Esther Rolle moment. St. Mark was and will always be special. During my bereavement period, I received a call from my favorite Sunday School Teacher from St. Mark. It wasn't the first time she called. She would frequently send me a text or call just to check on me and Mother. St. Mark would always show up as the same member who had purchased us a washing machine and dryer to eliminate our laundry mat trips, even called and offered her home for respite when I traveled to Orlando for Mother's funeral arrangements.

At the funeral, the family would wear white not just for Mother's maiden name but for her beauty, brilliance, purity and transparency. It was a moving and powerful homegoing service as we would even hear an electrifying eulogy from the AME Bishop who was her former pastor. Multiple times, we were brought to our feet as Mother's funeral service felt like an intense spiritual revival. When it was my time to speak, I offered reflections of who she was as a woman of God, and a mother. These were some of the words that I offered:

Mother learned how to drive late in life. As a matter of fact, she didn't learn how to drive until her 30s. She was a nervous driver. She drove slowly, carefully and she always took the street route never daring to drive on any freeway. As a child, living in the parsonage, whenever we would return from any trip or excursion, Mother would slowly pull in the garage, put the gear in park, breathe, and say "Thank You Jesus. We made it home." This was a habit for her. It was repetitive. She would pull into the car garage, breathe, and then say "Thank You Jesus. We made it home."

One day, I asked her, I said, "Mama, why do you always say that?"

She replied, "I have to thank God for allowing us to make it home safely. Anything could have happened to us out there. I must always give God thanks for his protection. When you get older, you'll know what I'm talking about."

Well, Mama, if you're listening, I'm a little older now so I understand. I've been through some things but I made it. I've experienced heartaches but through the grace of God I made it! Thank you Mama for those words! You made it! No more sickness! You made it! No more suffering! You made it! No more pain! You made it to a place where everyday is Sunday and Sabbath has no end! You made it! I'm happy for you Mama! I rejoice with you and I can shout it from the rooftops, "THANK YOU JESUS… MAMA MADE IT HOME!"

Indeed, it was our hope that in the heavenly realms, Mother was pleased with the funeral's outcome as she had now exchanged her cross for a crown.

If I completely had my way, I would've chosen Tupac Shakur's "Dear Mama" as a musical selection but in the traditionalism of Mother and the sacred space, it would've been inappropriate. In spite of how some may feel about Tupac as a man and a musician, most must admit that there is something transparent and authentic about the song, "Dear Mama." Along with hearing an artist, one hears the soul of a son who understands the struggle of a single mother and is blessed by her sacrifice. For anyone who was raised by a strong single mother, there is a connection somewhere in this song whose poignant lyrics speak to the single mother's fortitude. It certainly spoke to me in Mother's journey as I would find comfort in it during my private grief.

After the funeral, I would return to my work as a chaplain but the grief would move with me. There were clinical visits and supportive care team meetings where patients and families grappled with life and death decisions. Knowing their struggle more intimately, I sat in the same seat with Mother's situation.

Often, I would give family tours of the Hospice House and think of Mother in passing by the room where she died. One day, I walked by and saw a 'butterfly' on its door. It meant a soul had passed—flown away just as Mother had sometime earlier. I said a prayer for that family's strength as well as my own in remembrance of Mother. Carl Jung, the psychologist, had me pegged with his term 'wounded healer,' whereas I loved to help others heal for in turn I was being healed.

Years would past and time would move fast and forward while the grief of Mother would continue. Like Father's grief, it would travel in the oddest places. The hospital where I worked would regularly have an employee gift fair where various vendors would sell goods. During one of those fairs, I would be drawn to a vendor who sold angel ornaments. Soon, I would be joined by a unfamiliar employee whose attire told me that she worked in the dietary dept. We would hold casual conversation as we spoke in admiration of the beautifully decorative angels.

"They remind me of my mother!" the young lady said.

"Me too!" I delightfully responded.

"My mother passed in 2015," the young lady said.

"My mother passed in 2015 too," I responded.

"She died in April," the young lady sadfully said.

"My mother died in April of that year too." In responding slowly, I was feeling something unexplainable and by her facial response, she was feeling it too.

"She died April," but before she could say the date, we both said, "April 9, 2015."

Chills went through my body. Clearly, a higher power was at work here. With tears, we hugged tightly. What were the odds of two women, strangers from a different race and background meeting each other only to discover that our "angel" mothers share the same death anniversary.

Onlookers, unknown to our Kairos moment, paused and asked, "Is everything alright?"

"We're good," we said.

In trying to gather ourselves, we were good, forever connected as we would cross paths from time to time in the hospital. If not careful, grief can have you feeling like you're alone or that no one else in the world feels or understand your loss. Remember this. There's always someone who knows the kind of grief that you're going through and God will put them in your life just when you need them the most.

For many mornings before that and after that, the Shaws would watch *Good Times* as the theme song would blare from our television set. Esther Rolle's face would appear along with the rest of the television show's cast. In seeing Rolle's face, I didn't think anything of it. I didn't think anything of it.

Let the Church Say AMEN

The beginning of each new year comes new possibilities. 2018 would prove just that as we exchanged our Kansas City, Missouri residency with one in San Francisco, California. In first breaking the news to my Kansas City co-workers of the relocation, their response would be strange stares with open mouths.

An announcement of moving to one of the richest cities in the world is not typical which was why one of my co-workers blurted in jest, "What did you do, win the lottery!?"

We laughed at her humor but this was no luck.

Robert and I considered it a major blessing. It was a divine assignment as our bishop, a kind hearted soul with a giving spirit, promoted us to the oldest African American congregation in San Francisco, Bethel AME Church, in October 2017. We waited for our children to finish their fall semester of school in Kansas City before relocation. This would be our fourth church/city relocation in fifteen years.

When we first arrived in San Francisco, we were not only welcomed by The Golden Gate Bridge but the beauty and uniqueness of its splendid geography. There were spectacular oceans and mountain views along with diverse food and cultures.

Our children were welcomed with new things as well. They would now be introduced to the catholic school world in exchanging their public school free dress for a uniform. Robby, our son, was excited to be living in the city of his favorite NBA championship team while Raven, our daughter, was anxious about making new friends at school.

Robert and I were in still in awe that our lives had transitioned to this amazing place especially in driving past the Pacific Ocean.

"Ann… Are we living in San Francisco?" Robert would often ask.

"I think we are." This was my response in still finding it hard to believe that we now lived there.

Though San Francisco had its assets, it also had its agitations. It was challenging getting used to three types of trash organization systems (recyclable, organic, and sewage). For the vehicle driver, it was difficult locating city parking spaces and the traffic congestion would make the most patient person want to pull their hair out.

Our solace, however, would be our warm, congenial, beautiful new church, Bethel AME Church, whom we affectionately called "THE HOUSE" as their smiling faces, big hearts, and loving arms were constant. Our first Sunday worship service there was spirit-filled. The choir and congregation was responsive with shouts as Robert preached his sermon on a ladder. Their love and elation for the word of God even extended outside of its sanctuary to a community where it housed a homeless women's shelter and a food pantry.

In San Francisco, our family would once more live in a parsonage. This one offered opportunities for exercise with its 36 indoor steps that led to the top floor. For me, I would once more live in a no air condition house. These circumstances, however would be different from my childhood home in

Orlando, Florida. Homes in San Francisco doesn't have air condition because they don't need it. It's unnecessary when the city's average yearly weather is 65 degrees.

My first birthday in San Francisco would come with cards, cake, and gifts along with a text from George. He had sent a copy of my birth certificate along with a joke about my birth weight of ten pounds. My response was mere as I gave it little attention. About five minutes later, however, he would text me a birthday gift in the form of a picture that would stop me right in my tracks.

As I loudly gasped, "Oh my God!" my family huddled around as our eyes were fixated on the family picture that we took with Esther Rolle in December of 1979.

My children surprisingly inquired, "Mom! We didn't know you knew her!"

While Robert jokingly inquired, "Why are you the only one standing like this?" He then mimicked my stance as the only one on the picture with a hip lean.

We all laughed. My family was familiar with watching Esther Rolle on *Good Times* but unfamiliar to my personal connection with her. Life with all of its twists and turns had gradually removed the Esther Rolle memory from my mind, leaving Robert and the children uninformed of that fateful day.

In the shock of it all, I couldn't explain as I needed to contact George immediately.

"It took our picture with Esther Rolle for you to call me… huh?" George said when I called.

"You know it did!" was my rebuttal as we shared a moment of laughter. It was the same joy that we had when we both caught eye contact in watching Esther Rolle walk down the center aisle of St. Mark almost 40 years earlier.

It had been a really long time since George and I talked. We were both awkwardly aware of the moment due to our sibling disconnect. Our estranged relationship, however, hadn't always been that way. As youth, we would share relationship secrets and our love for music including the artist Prince. As an adult, George even imitated Prince's shoe game by wearing cowboy boot heels to boost his height. When I left my aunt and uncle's home, George allowed me to live with him and later, when he needed a place to stay, I returned the favor.

George was even there during one of my worst times— the rape. On that night, George was in the house as he was sound asleep in his closed door bedroom. When Mother and I awoke him to the horror, he was just as upset, even in disbelief.

"I didn't hear anything!" he yelled.

Before Father's arrival, George was my advocate. "We're going to get this m*****f*** who did this to you!" he declared as he hugged me.

George even went with Mother and Father to the hospital as they waited on me to complete the rape kit. Afterwards, he even stayed with Mother making sure she was alright before joining us in Jacksonville later that summer.

Not only in the worst of times but during our best moments, George and I were there for each other. George was the first to know that I was pregnant with my second child, even predicting his gender before any sonogram confirmed it.

"Hey Sis. I can't wait for Robby Jr. to get here!" he said.

"How do you know it's a boy G?!" I responded.

"Ahhh. Just trust me. You're having a boy!" George emphatically said.

Earlier in life, when George discovered that he was a father, I, too, shared in his joy.

"Hey Sis. Guess what. I'm a Father," George said.

"I'm happy for you Bro!" I said in response.

At times, we would argue but we would always eventually reconcile.

In recent years, this was not the case as our sibling relationship would grow more distant with disagreements and bickering, especially over Mother's care. This included sparring and spewing words at each other that were not befitting for anyone especially those of the holy cloth. Our sibling hostility even overflowed into Mother's funeral, yet we maintained civility for the respect of Mother and the sake of public face. In the three years since Mother had passed, our conversations were limited only to one line text and if seen at any family function, our engagement was brief.

With this sudden discovery of the picture, things would be different as George and I reminisced on that memorable visit from Esther Rolle including how her life evolved after her visit to our home. We talked about how she starred in the movie *Driving Miss Daisy,* in which she played a maid to a rich Jewish widow, and *Rosewood*, which was a movie about an African American Florida community in the 1920s that was attacked by a lynch mob.

"After *Good Times*, her life was low key but she still had a pretty good acting career," I said.

"Yeah," George said in response. "She's gone now. I think she died about 20 years ago or so."

It had been 20 years since Esther Rolle passed, and, as she requested, her funeral was held in her home church of Bethel AME Church, Pompano Beach, FL. Rolle's spirit brought American families together to watch her on the iconic television show *Good Times*. It would be the same spirit that would bring George and I back together, with help from Mother, of course, who saved the memory and picture just for us.

With all of our individual and family transitions over the years from house to house, city to city, Mother insisted that we keep the pictures for she always said, "They're going to be worth something one day." Over the years, the pictures traveled and were preserved making its way to the back of closets, relatives' garages and basements.

A few months after Mother passed, George and I met at our Uncle Clarence's townhome in southwest Atlanta to divvy up our picture inheritance. We seemingly looked at hundreds of pictures from deceased relatives, family reunions, high school proms, holidays, etc., but the picture with Esther Rolle was never observed. After hours of review, we placed them in boxes and left. George had now found this picture among his stash and now it was on my cell phone with Mother's earthly and eternal message still holding true.

From that moment, George and I communicated more over the next few months than we did in prior years. We would talk casually about family including Mother.

"You know sis, it doesn't matter how much work I do in the gym. I still can't get rid of these varicose veins that mama left me," George said.

I responded, "I inherited them too Bro! They just won't go away!" We both laughed and then grew quiet in thinking of Mother. Also, we spoke of Tymy, whom George would soon visit in Kansas City.

In later conversation, George and I would return to our Esther Rolle moment.

George said, "Things were so good then sis." After which, he cleared his throat, as he often did, when talking about something that was emotionally deep for him. He continued. "We were like kings and queens."

I then responded, "We still are Bro. We still are. We never stopped being kings and queens or even Champions."

With remembrance, sometimes, there's grief. Our lives had taken a strange turn from the glory days of Esther Rolle and St. Mark to the gory of life's struggles and hardships. George was right in that it felt like we were royalty in 1979, especially with a house visit from one of the most beloved and popular faces on television. The truth is we were still royalty even in our difficulties. As God's children and with God's grace, we had survived life's daunting challenges and even moreso a faltering sibling relationship which was now good and all was forgiven.

Often, I wonder why Christ's first word on the cross involved forgiveness. When you think about it, forgiveness is the one word that we need the most whether to 'give it' or 'receive it.'

George's visit with Tymy was soon realized as he would often call and inform me of their whereabouts. Over that weekend, George was excited as he would send text messages, pictures, and even leave voicemails when I missed his call.

The Monday following George's visit with Tymy would appear to be an ordinary one in San Francisco. There would be no cooking in recuperation from a long Sunday and even longer Monday. Robert and our son Robby would leave the house for dinner pick-up while our daughter Raven would stay behind. My cell phone would ring with George's name appearing as the contact. When answering, I assumed he had returned to Atlanta and would inform me of his visit with Tymy.

"What's up G?" I greeted, but the voice was not that of George.

"Hello...Hello," the stranger said.

Surprisingly, I emphatically responded, "Who is this... What's going on?" The stranger continued, "Ma'am I'm here at the gas station and there's a gentleman here. He's passed out on the car."

Known to be a prankster, I initially thought George was playing a joke but after awhile, it seemed as though something else was at play. Paranoia set in as I soon thought George had been robbed or kidnapped, but in continuing to investigate the stranger's integrity, I found him to be of good intentions. The stranger found my phone number from George's cell phone as I was one of the last persons that George recently contacted.

After being informed that the paramedics were on their way, the stranger sent a dagger to my heart, "He's not well ma'am. He's not well."

Immediately, there was a flood of tears and a familiarity with his choice of words that confirmed George's health status. As a healthcare chaplain, we were taught to use careful jargon in explaining to families the health condition of their loved ones, especially when the diagnosis was grim. Even when knowing the truth, we could never say it. The delivery and details of any medical information was left only to the physician in charge. In that moment, I needed the television sitcom *Amen* to shine on me because I was in a dark place regarding George's poor health. Only God's light could bring me out.

The airplane couldn't fly fast enough to Atlanta as I was both anxious and fearful in seeing George and speaking with the medical staff. Upon arriving at the hospital, my cousin Margo would meet me at the doors of the Neurological ICU to prepare me for what I would witness. It was unreal seeing George in this fragile state. His physical prowess always symbolized strength as his frame carried the likings of a bodybuilder. His career was that of a trainer as his function of ordained ministry was seen more than in a pulpit but a gym filled with the sounds of sacred steel iron weights. George would daily lift weights all the while encouraging others to push beyond their physical capabilities to be their best selves. Body strengthening and conditioning was the biggest thing in his life, where he was most committed. Even on that October evening, when the stranger found him passed out on his car at the gas station, George had just left the Cathedral's gym while training a woman for a bodybuilding competition. Though tired from his recent Kansas City visit, he forged on to coach her anyway. As I tearfully now witnessed him in this paralytic condition, his neurologist would inform me that his prognosis was poor.

For days, family and friends from the "Jesus Saves" Church, The Cathedral, and even St. Mark would offer prayers and words of encouragement, but there would be no physical improvements. As George lay there in the hospital bed, it was unfathomable to see him in this condition. George was always a fighter who overcame obstacles. He even graduated from Morris Brown College with a bachelor's degree in business administration at the age of 45. This was long after beginning college years earlier. George's journey gave credence to the adage, 'The race is not given to the swift nor to the strong but to the one who endures to the end.' Sadly, at the prime age of 50 years old, George's physical end would come.

When arriving at the funeral home to make arrangements, I was greeted by its aesthetics that included a chapel, baby grand piano, and monogrammed chairs with the letter 'L' that represented the first letter of the funeral home's name. Inside its space, the employees were dressed in fine clothing, drenched with southern hospitality and good manners, utilizing the respectful words 'ma'ams' and 'sirs,' which was a friendly reminder of why I loved Atlanta so much.

While sitting in the conference room, a kind, older, unfamiliar gentleman, who was the owner and proprietor, entered. "I was just talking about your father," he said. The funeral director continued to speak about how he met Father in the late 1960s when Father served as his pastor of a small church in Conyers, GA. At that time, George was a baby and

Mother was pregnant with Tymy. He went on to speak about how Father encouraged him to tithe, which is a biblical mandate that encourages believers to give one tenth of earnings to God in support of the church.

"From this principle, tithing. I've grown spiritually and financially as I now have a multi-million dollar business and one of the largest funeral homes in the southeast United States," he said.

I continued to listen and inquire. "If I'm not mistaken, my father pastored that church for less than two years."

He responded, "It doesn't take a long time to make a big impact on someone's life. Your father even married me and my wife during that time. We will soon celebrate our 50th Wedding Anniversary, and your mother was so sweet in giving us dishes for a wedding gift which we still have today. They were really good people."

The funeral director's words were comforting as it spoke of my parents' good nature and character, making for a memorable, lasting impression. Instead of them feeling far away, it reminded me of how close they were, not only to myself but to others.

In preparation for George's funeral, there was somebody else whose presence was also required, Tymy. Being in charge of her care, I left Atlanta temporarily and traveled to Kansas City in order to help pack Tymy's things for George's funeral. She had just seen George alive two weeks earlier so she was still stunned over his loss. On our way to the airport, we had a moment.

"I'm angry," Tymy said.

When she said how she felt, it caught me off guard. Tymy was always closed with her feelings. In the past, I had inquired of her feelings in the loss of Mother and Father but I was unable to acquire any substantive information. This expression was surprising and groundbreaking.

"Angry," I said in response.

Tymy sighed heavily and said, "Yes Clara! (My middle name that family and Orlando friends call me) I'm angry! I'm angry that George died!"

"I'm angry too Sis. I'm angry too," I said.

Tymy expressed what I've been feeling too 'anger.' When it comes to bereavement, we talk about the sadness way more than the anger part of it. It can be the 'if a loved one would've done something different then maybe the death would not have happened' situation. This was my feeling. George was not compliant with his blood pressure medication. If he would've taken his medicine, I thought, then maybe he wouldn't have suffered a massive stroke and died. Anger can leave us with so many 'ifs,' 'whys,' or 'maybes' as if our loved ones death could have been avoided. The truth of the matter is George's time on earth was set and there was nothing I could do about it. I couldn't control death. If I could, George, like Mother and Father would still be alive.

After agreeing with Tymy over the anger issue, I took her hand and continued. "Listen sis. I'm angry too that George is gone. I miss him already. This is tough but we're going to get through this together… Alright?"

"Alright," Tymy said.

Just like at Father's funeral, Mother's funeral and now George's, Tymy and myself, along with other family, tried to get through it as we took our place on the bereaved family pew. Instead of St. Mark, we held George's services at St. Philip AME Church 'The Cathedral' in Atlanta, the church where he had been a member for twenty years. Again, we heard the uplifting music, remarks, and the words of comfort all while being embraced by Atlanta family, friends, and even St. Mark who were there through it all including our Esther Rolle moment.

After George's funeral, the grief process was in full swing. It was still so unbelievable that he was gone, especially after the the mending of our relationship. My mind reflected on the last conversation that I had with him. At the end of our conversation, I said the three words that hadn't been said in a long time, "I love you," when George suddenly hung up the phone. Afterwards, I wasn't sure whether George heard my "I love you" or if he loved me too. Later on, I listened to my voicemail.

This is what George said: "Hey sis! What's going on? Just checking in. Me and Tymy are leaving the movie theater. We just went to see *Night School.* Kevin Hart and Tiffany Haddish are hilarious! You got to go see it. Well. Gotta Go. Talk to you later! Love you!"

My heart smiled as George said, "I love you." His voice and message gave me a sweet peace in knowing that he loved me too. He loved me too.

Thanksgiving would soon come as families all over America would come together to be grateful for each other and the good food that they were about to receive. As the

Shaws gathered around the dining room table in the Bethel San Francisco parsonage, there was a void as my mind would be on George whom we just funeralized a month earlier. My attention was constantly drawn to my cell phone which held the family picture with Esther Rolle. It was the same picture that George sent me on my birthday. In looking across our dining room table, I realized that Tymy was not privy to the Esther Rolle photograph, yet her posture and smile was framed in the same pictorial moment as the rest of the Champions. Soon, I beckoned for her to come to the kitchen. As we sat at the kitchen bar, I leaned over to show her the cell phone picture and said, "Hey Sis. Remember This."

Of course, she did. In our remembrance, we laughed and talked about the good time we had in hopes of more good times to come.

PICTURE THIS EPILOGUE

Our family moment with *Good Times* actress Esther Rolle is not only pictured in a frame but in the heart. Her endearing presence blessed a clergy family with happiness and created a sweet memory. Its worth would compel a loving mother to keep it and treasure it. As a result, it would reunite and repair her son and daughter's withered relationship. Power still generates from this picture. It touches every part of my every being and it places me back to that faithful Sunday where we experienced one of our best times.

What is the condition of your family relationships? Where are the moments that have brought you the greatest joys or have they been overshadowed by the worst pains that have kept you and loved ones apart. After reading this book, it is my prayer that you take time and opportunity to reconnect with family. May you listen, talk, and heal from those wounds that have kept you separated and torn from one another. Let it be a starting point in reconciliation to something big, beautiful—family that will not only have a lasting impression for the present but for generations to come. Try it today. What is its worth? You might ask. Priceless.

ACKNOWLEDGEMENTS

To the Author of my Life: Jesus Christ, who offers FAVOR and FORGIVENESS every day and whose guidance, faithfulness, and undying love enabled me to complete this work.

To My Family: My husband, best friend and endless love, **Rev. Robert Ryland Shaw, II,** who was my first reader and biggest cheerleader during this process. Our amazing children, **Raven Noel Lovelace** and **Robert Ryland III,** whose love, suggestions, and encouragement have meant the world to me. My uncle, **Clarence Dean White,** who believed in this memoir from the very start and who served as a reader, staunch supporter and advisor.

To My Episcopal Leadership: Bishop Clement W. Fugh and **Episcopal Supervisor Alexia Butler Fugh** for your blessings on this endeavor.

To Bishop Anne Henning Byfield: Your Foreword was most timely and significant.

To Gatekeepers Press: Rob (President), **Tricia** (Author Manager), and **Tia** (Editor) for your constructive criticism and patience to ensure that I put forth my BEST work.

To **Dr. Bill Clark (deceased), Rev. Sharon D. Moore, Rev. Eddie Harris, Dr. Priscilla Dowden-White** and all other prophets who spoke this book into existence long before its conception.

Lastly, To those countless lives who have crossed my path. That moment in time has contributed to who I am today, **THANK YOU.** And to those lives who will be changed after reading this book, **THANK GOD.**